Anarcho-syndicalism: Theory and Practice

An Introduction to a Subject Which the Spanish War Has Brought into Overwhelming Prominence

Rudolf Rocker

1938

Contents

Chapter 1. Anarchism: Its Aims and Purposes — 3

Chapter 2. The Proletariat and the Beginning of the Modern Labour Movement — 15

Chapter 3. The Forerunners of Syndicalism — 25

Chapter 4. The Objectives of Anarchosyndicalism — 37

Chapter 5. The Methods of Anarcho-Syndicalism — 50

Chapter 6. The Evolution of Anarcho-Syndicalism — 60

Chapter 1. Anarchism: Its Aims and Purposes

Anarchism versus economic monopoly and state power; Forerunners of modern Anarchism; William Godwin and his work on Political Justice; P.J. Proudhon and his ideas of political and economic decentralisation; Max Stirner's work, The Ego and Its Own; M. Bakunin the Collectivist and founder of the Anarchist movement; P. Kropotkin the exponent of Anarchist Communism and the philosophy of Mutual Aid; Anarchism and revolution; Anarchism a synthesis of Socialism and Liberalism; Anarchism versus economic materialism and Dictatorship; Anarchism and the state; Anarchism a tendency of history; Freedom and culture.

Anarchism is a definite intellectual current in the life of our times, whose adherents advocate the abolition of economic monopolies and of all political and social coercive institutions within society. In place of the present capitalistic economic order Anarchists would have a free association of all productive forces based upon co-operative labour, which would have as its sole purpose the satisfying of the necessary requirements of every member of society, and would no longer have in view the special interest of privileged minorities within the social union.

In place of the present state organisation with their lifeless machinery of political and bureaucratic institutions Anarchists desire a federation of free communities which shall be bound to one another by their common economic and social interest and shall arrange their affairs by mutual agreement and free contract.

Anyone who studies at all profoundly the economic and social development of the present social system will easily recognise that these objectives do not spring from the Utopian ideas of a few imaginative innovators, but that they are the logical outcome of a thorough examination of the present-day social maladjustments, which with every new phase of the existing social conditions manifest themselves more plainly and more unwholesomely. Modern monopoly, capitalism and the totalitarian state are merely the last terms in a development which could culminate in no other results.

The portentous development of our present economic system, leading to a mighty accumulation of social wealth in the hands of privileged minorities and to a continuous impoverishment of the great masses of the people, prepared the way for the present political and social reaction. and befriended it in every way. It sacrificed the general interest of human society to the private interest of individuals, and thus systematically undermined the relationship between man and man. People forgot that industry is not an end in itself, but should only be a means to ensure to man his material subsistence and to make accessible to him the blessings of a higher intellectual culture. Where industry is everything and man is nothing begins the realm of a ruthless economic despotism whose workings are no less disastrous than those of any political despotism. The two mutually augment one another, and they are fed from the same source.

The economic dictatorship of the monopolies and the political dictatorship of the totalitarian state are the outgrowth of the same political objectives, and the directors of both have the presumption to try to reduce all the countless expressions of social life to the mechanical tempo of the machine and to tune everything organic to the lifeless machine of the political apparatus. Our modern social system has split the social organism in every country into hostile classes internally, and externally it has broken the common cultural circle up into hostile nations; and both classes and nations confront one another with open antagonism and by their ceaseless warfare keep the communal social life in continual convulsions. The late World War and its terrible after effects, which are themselves only the results of the present struggles for economic and political power, are only the logical consequences of this unendurable condition, which will inevitably lead us to a universal catastrophe if social development does not take a new course soon enough. The mere fact that most states are obliged today to spend from fifty to seventy percent of their annual income for so-called national defence and the liquidation of old war debts is proof of the untenability of the present status, and should make clear to everybody that the alleged protection which the state affords the individual is certainly purchased too dearly.

The ever growing power of a soulless political bureaucracy which supervises and safeguards the life of man from the cradle to the grave is putting ever greater obstacles in the way of the solidaric co-operation of human beings and crushing out every possibility of new development. A system which in every act of its life sacrifices the welfare of large sections of the people, yes, of whole nations, to the selfish lust for power and the economic interests of small minorities must of necessity dissolve all social ties and lead to a constant war of all against all. This system has been merely the pacemaker for the great intellectual and social reaction which finds its expression today in modern Fascism, far surpassing the obsession for power of the absolute monarchy of past centuries and seeking to bring every sphere of human activity under the control of the state. Just as for the various systems of religious theology, God is everything and man nothing, so for this modern political theology, the state is everything and the man nothing. And just as behind the "will of God" there always lay hidden the will of privileged minorities, so today there hides behind the "will of the state" only the selfish interest of those who feel called to interpret this will in their own sense and to force it upon the people.

Anarchist ideas are to be found in every period of known history, although there still remains a good deal of work for historical work in this field. We encounter them in the Chinese sage, Lao-Tse (The Course and The Right Way) and in the later Greek philosophers, the Hedonists and Cynics and other advocates of so-called "natural right," and in particular in Zeno who, at the opposite pole from Plato, founded the Stoic school. They found expression in the teaching of the Gnostic, Karpocrates, in Alexandria, and had an unmistakable influence on certain Christian sects of the Middle Ages in France, Germany and Holland, almost all of which fell victims to the most savage persecutions. In the history of the Bohemian reformation they found a powerful champion in Peter Chelcicky, who in his work, "The Net of Faith," passed the same judgement on the church and the state as Tolstoy did later. Among the great humanists there was Rabelais, who in his description of the happy Abbey of Thélème (Gargantua) presented a picture of life freed from all authoritarian restraints. Of other pioneers of libertarian thinking we will mention here only La Boétie, Sylvan Maréchal, and, above all, Diderot, in whose voluminous writings one finds thickly strewn the utterances of a truly great mind which had rid itself of every authoritarian prejudice.

Meanwhile, it was reserved for more recent history to give clear form to the anarchist perception of life and to connect it with the immediate processes of social evolution. This was done for the first time in William Godwin's splendidly conceived work, *Concerning Political Justice and its Influence upon General Virtue and Happiness*, London, 1793. Godwin's work was, we might say, the ripened fruit of that long evolution of the concepts of political and social radicalism in England which proceeds in a continuous line from George Buchanan through Richard Hooker, Gerard Winstanley, Algernon Sidney, John Locke, Robert Wallace and John Bellers to Jeremy Bentham, Joseph Priestley, Richard Price and Thomas Paine.

Godwin recognised very clearly that the cause of social evils is to be sought, not in the form of the state, but in its very existence. Just as the state presents only a caricature of a genuine society, so also it makes of human beings who are held under its eternal guardianship merely caricatures of their real selves by constantly compelling them to repress their natural inclinations and holding them to things that are repugnant to their inner impulses. Only in this way is it possible to mould human beings to the established form of good subjects. A normal human being who was not interfered with in his natural development would of himself shape the environment that suits his inborn demand for peace and freedom.

But Godwin also recognised that human beings can only live together naturally and freely when the proper economic conditions for this are given, and when the individual is no longer subject to exploitation by another, a consideration which the representatives of mere political radicalism almost completely overlooked. Hence they were later compelled to make consistently greater concessions to that power of the state which they had wished to restrict to a minimum. Godwin's idea of a stateless society assumed the social ownership of all natural and social wealth, and the carrying on of economic life by the free co-operation of the producers; in this sense he was really the founder of the later communist Anarchism.

Godwin's work had a very strong influence on advanced circles of the English workers and the more enlightened sections of the liberal intelligentsia. Most important of all, he contributed to give to the young socialist movement in England, which found its maturest exponents in Robert Owen, John Gray and William Thompson, that unmistakable libertarian character which it had for a long time, and which it never assumed in Germany and many other countries.

But a far greater influence on the development of Anarchist theory was that of Pierre-Joseph Proudhon, one of the most intellectually gifted and certainly the most many-sided writer of whom modern socialism can boast. Proudhon was completely rooted in the intellectual and social life of his period, and these inspired his attitude upon every question he dealt with. Therefore, he is not to be judged, as he has been by even by many of his later followers, by his special practical proposals, which were born of the needs of the hour. Amongst the numerous socialist thinkers of his time he was the one who understood most profoundly the cause of social maladjustment, and possessed, besides, the greatest breadth of vision. He was the outspoken opponent of all systems, and saw in social evolution the eternal urge to new and higher forms of intellectual and social life, and it was his conviction that this evolution could not be bound by any abstract general formulas.

Proudhon opposed the influence of the Jacobin tradition, which dominated the thinking of the French democrats and of most of the Socialists of that period with the same determination as the interference of the central state and economic policy in the natural processes of social advance. To rid society of these two cancerous growths was for him the great task of the nineteenth-century revolution. Proudhon was no communist. He condemned property as merely the privilege of exploitation, but he recognised the ownership of the instruments of production by all, made effective by industrial groups bound to one another by free contract, so long as this right was not made to serve the exploitation of others and as long as the full product of his individual labour was assured to every human being. This organisation based on reciprocity (mutualité) guarantees the enjoyment of equal rights by each in exchange for equal services. The average working time required for the completion of any product becomes the measure of its value and is the basis of mutual exchange. In this way capital is deprived of its usurial power and is completely bound up with the performance of work. By being made available to all it ceases to be an instrument for exploitation.

Such a form of economy makes an political coercive apparatus superfluous. Society becomes a league of free communities which arrange their affairs according to need, by themselves or in association with others, and in which man's freedom finds in the freedom of others not its limitation, but its security and confirmation. "The freer, the more independent and enterprising the individual is in a society, the better for the society." This organisation of Federalism in which Proudhon saw the immediate future sets no definite limitations on further possibilities of development, and offers the widest scope to every individual and social activity. Starting out from this point of view of the federation, Proudhon combated likewise the aspirations for political activity of the awakening nationalism of the time, and in particular that nationalism which found in Mazzini, Garibaldi, Lelewel, and others, such strong advocates. In this respect also he saw more clearly than most of his contemporaries. Proudhon exerted a strong influence on the development of socialism, which made itself felt especially in the Latin countries. But the so-called individual Anarchism, which found able exponents in America in such men as Josiah Warren, Stephen Pearl Andrews, William B. Greene, Lysander Spooner, Francis D. Tandy, and most notably in Benjamin R. Tucker ran in similar lines, though none of its representatives could approach Proudhon's breadth of view.

Anarchism found a unique expression in Max Stirner's (Johann Kaspar Schmidt's) book, *Der Einzige und sein Eigentum* (The Ego and His Own), which, it is true, quickly passed into oblivion and had no influence at all on the Anarchist movement as such — though it was to experience an unexpected resurrection fifty years later. Stirner's book is pre-eminently a philosophical work which traces man's dependence on so-called higher powers through all its devious ways, and is not timid about drawing inferences from the knowledge gained by the survey. It is the book of a conscious and deliberate insurgent, which reveals no reverence for any authority, however exalted, and therefore impels powerfully to independent thinking.

Anarchism found a virile champion of vigorous revolutionary energy in Michael Bakunin, who took his stand upon the teachings of Proudhon, but extended them on the economic side when he, along with the collectivist wing of the First International, came out for the collective ownership of the land and of all other means of production, and wished to restrict the right of private ownership to the full product of individual labour. Bakunin also was an opponent of Communism, which in his time had a thoroughly authoritarian character, like that which it has again assumed today in Bolshevism. In one of his four speeches at the Congress of the *League of Peace and Freedom* in Bern (1868), he said: "I am not a Communist because Communism unites all forces of society in the state and becomes absorbed in it; because it inevitably leads to the concentration of all property in the hands of the state, while I seek the abolition of the state — the complete elimination of the principle of authority and governmental guardianship, which under the pretence of making men moral and civilising them, has up to now always enslaved, oppressed, exploited and ruined them."

Bakunin was a determined revolutionary and did no believe in an amicable adjustment of the existing class conflict. He recognised that the ruling classes blindly and stubbornly opposed even the slightest social reform, and accordingly saw the only salvation in an international social revolution, which should abolish all the ecclestical, political, military, bureaucratic and judicial institutions of the existing social system and introduce in their stead a federation of free workers' associations to provide for the requirements of daily life. Since he, like so many of his contemporaries, believed in the close proximity of the revolution, he directed all his vast energy to combine all the genuinely revolutionary and libertarian elements within and without the *International* to safeguard the coming revolution against any dictatorship or retrogression to the old conditions. Thus he became in a very special sense the reator of the modern Anarchist movement.

Anarchism found a valuable advocate in Peter Kropotkin, who set himself the task of making the achievements of modern natural science available for the development of the sociological concepts of Anarchism. In his ingenious book *Mutual Aid — a Factor of Evolution*, he entered the lists against so-called *Social Darwinism*, whose exponents tried to prove the inevitability of the existing social conditions from the Darwinian theory of the struggle for existence by raising the struggle of the strong against the weak to the status of an iron law for all natural processes, to which even man is subject. In reality this conception was strongly influenced by the Malthusian doctrine that life's table is not spread for all, and that the unneeded will just have to reconcile themselves to this fact.

Kropotkin showed that this conception of nature as a field of unrestricted warfare is only a caricature of real life, and that along with the brutal struggle for existence, which is fought out with tooth and claw, there exists in nature another principle which is expressed in the social combination of the weaker species and the maintenance of races by the evolution of social instincts and mutual aid.

In this sense man is not the creator of society, but society is the creator of man, for he inherited from the that preceded him the social instinct which alone enabled him to maintain himself in his first environment against the physical superiority of other species, and to make sure of an undreamed-of height of development. This second tendency in the struggle for existence is far superior to the first, as is shown by the steady retrogression of those species which have no social life and are dependent merely upon their physical strength. This view, which today is meeting with consistently wider acceptance in the natural sciences and in social research, opened wholly new vistas to speculation concerning human evolution.

The fact is that even under the worst despotism most of man's personal relations with his fellows are arranged by free agreement and solidaric co-operations, without which social life would not be possible at all. If this were not the case even the strongest coercive arrangements of the state would not be able to maintain the social order for a single day. However, these natural forms of behaviour, which arise from man's inmost nature, are today constantly interfered with and crippled by the effects of economic exploitation and governmental guardianship, which represents in human society the brutal form of the struggle for existence, which has to be overcome by the other form of mutual aid and free co-operation. The consciousness of personal responsibility and that other precious good that has come down to man by inheritance from remote antiquity: that capacity for sympathy with others in which all social ethics, all ideas of social justice, have their origin, develop best in freedom.

Like Bakunin, Kropotkin too was a revolutionary. But he, like Élisée Reclus and others, saw in revolution only a special phase of the evolutionary process, which appears when new social aspirations are so restricted in their natural development by authority that they have to shatter the old shell by violence before they can function as new factors in human life. In contrast to

Proudhon and Bakunin, Kropotkin advocated community ownership, not only of the means of production, but of the products of labour as well, as it was his opinion that in the present status of technique no exact measure of the value of individual labour is possible, but that, on the other hand, by a rational direction of our modern methods of labour it will be possible to assure comparative abundance to every human being. Communist Anarchism, which before him had already been urged by Joseph Dejacque, Élisée Reclus, Errico Malatesta, Carlo Cafiero, and others, and which is advocated by the great majority of Anarchists today, found in him one of its most brilliant exponents.

Mention must also be made here of Leo Tolstoy, who took from primitive Christianity and, on the basis of the ethical principles laid down in the gospels, arrived at the idea of a society without rulership.[1]

Common to all Anarchists is the desire to free society of all political and social coercive institutions which stand in the way of development of a free humanity. In this sense Mutualism, Collectivism and Communism are not to be regarded as closed systems permitting no further development, but merely as economic assumptions as to the means of safeguarding a free community. There will even probably be in society of the future different forms of economic co-operation operating side by side, since any social progress must be associated with that free experiment and practical testing out for which in a society of free communities there will be afforded every opportunity.

The same holds true for the various methods of Anarchism. Most Anarchists of our time are convinced that a social transformation of society cannot be brought about without violent revolutionary convulsions. The violence of these convulsions, of course, depends upon the strength of the resistance which the ruling classes will be able to oppose to the realisation of the new ideas. The wider the circles which are inspired with the idea of a reorganisation of society in the spirit of freedom and Socialism, the easier will be the birth pains of the coming social revolution.

In modern anarchism we have the confluence of the two great currents which during and since the French Revolution have found such characteristic expression in the intellectual life of Europe: Socialism and Liberalism. Modern Socialism developed when profound observers in social life came to see more and more clearly that political constitutions and changes in the form of government could never get to the bottom of that great problem that we call "the social question." Its supporters recognised that a social equalising of human beings , despite the loveliest of theoretical assumptions, is not possible so long as people are separated into classes on the basis of their owning or not owning property, classes whose mere existence excludes in advance any thought of a genuine community. And so there developed the recognition that only by elimination of economic monopolies and common ownership of the means of production, in a word, by a complete transformation of all economic conditions and social institutions associated with them, does a condition of social justice become thinkable, a status in which society shall become a genuine community, and human labour shall no longer serve the ends of exploitation, but shall serve to assure abundance to everyone. But as soon as Socialism began to assemble its forces and became a movement, there at once came to light certain differences of opinion due to the influence of the social environment in different countries. It is a fact that every political concept from theocracy to Cæsarism and dictatorship have affected certain factions in the Socialist movement.

---

[1] The reader will find in the works of Max Nettlau listed in the bibliography a very well informed hisory of Anarchist doctrines and movements.

Meanwhile, there have been two great currents in political thought which have been of decisive significance for the development of Socialistic ideals: Liberalism, which powerfully stimulated advanced minds in the Anglo-Saxon countries and Spain, in particular, and Democracy in the later sense to which Rousseau gave expression in his *Social Contract*, and which found its most influential representatives in French Jacobinism. While liberation in its social theorising started off from the individual and wished to limit the state's activities to a minimum, Democracy took its stand on an abstract collective concept, Rousseau's "general will," which it sought to fix in the national state.

Liberalism and Democracy were preeminently political concepts, and since the great majority of the original adherents of both maintained the right of ownership in the old sense, these had to renounce them both when economic development took a course which could not be practically reconciled with the original principles of Democracy, and still less with those of Liberalism. Democracy, with its motto of "all citizens equal before the law," and Liberalism with its "right of man over his own person," both shipwrecked on the realities of the capitalist economic form. So long as millions of human beings in every country had to sell their labour-power to a small minority of owners, and to sink into the most wretched misery if they could find no buyers, the so-called "equality before the law" remains merely a pious fraud, since the laws are made by those who find themselves in possession of the social wealth. But in the same way there can also be no talk of a "right over one's own person," for that right ends when one is compelled to submit to the economic dictation of another if he does not want to starve.

Anarchism has in common with Liberalism the idea that the happiness and prosperity of the individual must be the standard of all social matters. And, in common with the great representatives of Liberal thought, it has also the idea of limiting the functions of government to a minimum. Its supporters have followed this thought to its ultimate logical consequences, and wish to eliminate every institution of political power from the life of society. When Jefferson clothes the basic concept of Liberalism in the words: "that government is best which governs least," then Anarchists say with Thoreau: "That government is best which governs not at all."

In common with the founders of socialism, Anarchists demand the abolition of all economic monopolies and the common ownership of the soil and all other means of production, the use of which must be available for all without distinction; for personal and social freedom is conceivable only on the basis of equal economic advantages for everybody. Within the socialist movement itself the Anarchists represent the viewpoint that the war against capitalism must be at the same time a war against all institutions of political power, for in history economic exploitation has always gone hand in hand with political and social oppression. The exploitation of man by man and the dominion of man over man are inseparable, and each is the condition of the other.

As long as within society a possessing and a non-possessing group of human beings face one another in enmity, the state will be indispensable to the possessing minority for the protection of its privileges. When this condition of social injustice vanishes to give place to a higher order of things, which shall recognise no special rights and shall have as its basic assumption the community of social interests, government over men must yield the field to the to the administration of economic and social affairs, or to speak with Saint-Simon: "The time will come when the art of governing man will disappear. A new art will take its place, the art of administering things."

And his disposes of the theory maintained by Marx and his followers that the state, in the form of a proletarian dictatorship, is a necessary transitional stage to a classless society, in which the state after the elimination of all class conflicts and then of classes themselves, will dissolve itself and vanish from the canvas. This concept, which completely mistakes the real nature of the state and the significance in history of the factor of political power, is only the logical outcome of so-called economic materialism, which sees in all the phenomena of history merely the inevitable effects of the methods of production of the time. Under the influence of this theory people came to regard the different forms of the state and all other social institutions as a "juridical and political superstructure" on the "economic edifice" of society, and thought that they had found in that theory the key to every historical process. In reality every section of history affords us thousands of examples of the way in which the economic development of a country has been set back for centuries and forced into prescribed forms by particular struggles for political power.

Before the rise of the ecclesiastical monarchy Spain was industrially the most advanced country in Europe and held the first place in economic production in almost every field. But a century after the triumph of the Christian monarchy most of its industries had disappeared. What was left of then survived only in the most wretched conditions. In most industries they had reverted to the most primitive methods of production. Agriculture collapsed, canals and waterways fell into ruin, and vast stretches of country were transformed into deserts. Down to this day Spain has never recovered from that setback. The aspirations of a particular caste for political power had laid economic development fallow for centuries.

Princely absolutism in Europe, with its silly "economic ordinances" and "industrial legislation," which punished severely any deviation from the prescribed methods of production and permitted no new inventions, blocked industrial progress in European countries for centuries, and prevented its natural development. And were there not considerations of political power which after the World War constantly balked any escape from the universal economic crisis and delivered the future of whole countries to politics-playing generals and political adventurers? Who will assert that modern Fascism was an inevitable result of economic development?

In Russia, however, where the so-called "proletarian dictatorship" has ripened into reality, the aspirations of a particular party for political power have prevented any truly socialistic reconstruction of economy and have forced the country into the slavery of a grinding state-capitalism. The "dictatorship of the proletariat," in which naive souls wish to see merely a passing, but inevitable, transition stage to real Socialism, has today grown into a frightful despotism, which lags behind the tyranny of the Fascist states in nothing.

The assertion that the state must continue to exist until class conflicts, and classes with them, disappear, sounds, in the light of all historical experience, almost like a bad joke. Every type of political power presupposes some particular form of human slavery, for the maintenance of which it is called into being. Just as outwardly, that is, in relation to other states, the state has to create certain artificial antagonisms in order to justify its existence, so also internally the cleavage of society into castes, ranks, and classes is an essential condition of its continuance. The state is capable only of protecting old privileges and creating new ones; in that its whole significance is exhausted.

A new state which has been brought into existence by a social revolution can put an end to the privileges of the old ruling classes, but it can do this only by immediately setting up a new privileged class, which it will require for the maintenance of its rulership. The development of the Bolshevist bureaucracy in Russia under the alleged dictatorship of the proletariat — which has never been anything but the dictatorship of a small clique *over* the proletariat and the entire Russian people — is merely a new instance of an old historical experience which has repeated itself uncountable times. This new ruling class, which today is rapidly growing into a new aristocracy, is set apart from the great masses of Russian peasants and workers just as clearly as are the privileged castes and classes in other countries from the mass of their peoples.

It could perhaps be objected that the new Russian commisar-ocracy cannot be put up on the same footing as the powerful financial and industrial oligarchies of capitalist states. But the objection will not hold. It is not the size or the extent of the privilege that matters, but its immediate effect on the daily life of the average human being. An American working man who, under moderately decent working conditions, earns enough to feed, clothe and house himself humanely and has enough left over to provide himself with some cultured enjoyments, feels the possession of millions by the Mellons and Morgans less than a man who earns hardly enough to satisfy his most urgent necessities [and who] feels the privileges of a little caste of bureaucrats, even if these are not millionaires. People who can scarcely get enough dry bread to satisfy their hunger, who live in squalid rooms which they are often obliged to share with strangers, and who, on top of this, are compelled to work under an intensified speed-up system which raises their productive capacity to the utmost, can but feel the privileges of an upper class which lacks nothing, much more keenly than their class comrades in capitalist countries. And this situation becomes still more unbearable when a despotic state denies to the lower classes the right to complain of existing conditions, so that any protest is made at the risk of their lives.

But even a far greater degree of economic equality than exists in Russia would still be no guarantee against political and social oppression. It is just this which Marxism and all the other schools of authoritarian Socialism have never understood. Even in prison, in the cloister or in the barracks one finds a fairly high degree of economic equality, as all the inmates are provided with the same dwelling, the same food, the same uniform and the same tasks. The ancient Inca state in Peru and the Jesuit state in Paraguay had brought equal economic provision for every inhabitant to a fixed system, but in spite of this the vilest despotism prevailed there, and the human being was merely the automaton of a higher will, on whose decisions he had not the slightest influence. It was not without reason that Proudhon saw in a "Socialism" without freedom the worst from of slavery. The urge for social justice can only develop properly and be effective when it grows out of man's sense of personal freedom and is based on that. In other words *Socialism will be free or it will not be at all.* In its recognition of this lies the genuine and profound justification for the existence of Anarchism.

Institutions serve the same purpose in the life of society as bodily organs do in plants or animals: they are the organs of the social body. Organs do not rise arbitrarily, but because of the definite necessities of the physical and social environment. The eye of a deep-sea fish is formed very differently from that of an animal that lives on land, because it has to satisfy quite different demands. Changed conditions of life produce changed organs, but the organ always performs the function it was evolved to perform, or a related one. And it gradually disappears or becomes rudimentary as soon as its function is no longer necessary to the organism. But an organ never takes on a function that does not accord with its proper purpose.

The same is true of social institutions. They, too, do not rise arbitrarily, but are called into being by special social needs to serve definite purposes. In this way this modern state was evolved after monopoly economy, and the class divisions associated with them had begun to make themselves more and more conspicuous in the framework of the old social order. The newly arise possessing classes had need of a political instrument of power to maintain their economic and social privileges over the masses of their own people, and to impose them from without on other groups of human beings. Thus arose the appropriate social conditions for the evolution of the modern state, as the organ of political power of privileged castes and classes for the forcible subjugation and oppression of the non-possessing classes. This task is the political lifework of the state, the essential reason for it existing at all. And to this task it has always remained faithful, must remain faithful, for it cannot escape from its skin.

Its external forms have altered in the course of its historical development, but its functions have always remained the same. They have even been constantly broadened in just the measure in which its supporters have succeeded in making further fields of social activity subservient to their needs. Whether the state be monarchy or republic, whether historically it is anchored to autocracy or in a national constitution, its function remains always the same. And just as the functions of the bodily organs of plants and animals cannot be arbitrarily altered, so that, for example, one cannot at will hear with his eyes and see with his ears, so also one cannot at pleasure transform an organ of social oppression into an instrument for the liberation of the oppressed. The state can only be what it is: the defender of mass exploitation and social privileges, the creator of privileged classes and castes and of new monopolies. Who fails to recognise this function of the state does not understand the real nature of the present social order at all, and is incapable of pointing out to humanity new outlooks for its social evolution.

Anarchism is no patent solution for all human problems, no Utopia of a perfect social order, as it has so often been called, since on principle it rejects all absolute schemes and concepts. It does not believe in any absolute truth, or in definite final goals for human development, but in an unlimited perfectibility of social arrangements and human living conditions, which are always straining after higher forms of expression, and to which for this reason one can assign no definite terminus nor set any fixed goal. The worst crime of any type of state is just that it always tries to force the rich diversity of social life into definite forms and adjust it to one particular form, which allows for no wider outlook and regards the previously exciting status as finished. The stronger its supporters feel themselves, the more completely they succeed in bringing every field of social life into their service, the more crippling is their influence on the operation of all creative cultural forces, the more unwholesomely does it affect the intellectual and social development of any particular epoch.

The so-called totalitarian state, which now rests like a mountain-weight upon whole peoples and tries to mould every expression of their intellectual and social life to the lifeless pattern set by a political providence, suppresses with ruthless and brutal force every effort at alteration of the existing conditions. The totalitarian state is a dire omen for our time, and shows with frightful clarity whither such a return to the barbarity of past centuries must lead. It is the triumph of the political machine over mind, the rationalising of human thought, feeling and behaviour according to the established rules of the officials. It is consequently the end of all intellectual culture.

Anarchism recognises only the relative significance of ideas, institutions and social forms. It is therefore not a fixed, self-enclosed social system, but rather a definite trend in the historic development of mankind, which, in contrast with the intellectual guardianship of all clerical and governmental institutions, strives for the free unhindered unfolding of all the individual and social forces in life. Even freedom is only a relative, not an absolute concept, since it tends constantly to become broader and affect wider circles in more manifold ways. For the Anarchist, freedom is not an abstract philosophical concept, but the vital concrete possibility for every human being to bring to full development all the powers, capacities and talents with which nature has endowed him, and turn them to social account. The less this natural development of man is influenced by ecclesiastical or political guardianship, the more efficient and harmonious will human personality become, the more will it become the measure of the society in which it has grown.

This is the reason why all great culture periods in history have been periods of political weakness. And that is quite natural, for political systems are always set upon the mechanising and not upon the organic development of social forces. State and culture are in the depth of their being irreconcilable opposites. Nietzsche recognised this very clearly when he wrote:

> "No one can finally spend more than he has. That holds good for individuals; it holds good for peoples. If one spends oneself for power, for high politics, for husbandry, for commerce, parliamentarism, military interests — if one gives away that amount of reason, earnestness, will, self-mastery, which constitutes one's real self for one thing, he will not have it for the other. Culture and the state — let no one be deceived about this — are antagonists: the 'Culture State' is merely a modern idea. The one lives on the other, the one prospers at the expense of the other. All great periods of culture are periods of political decline. Whatever is great in a cultured sense is non political, is even anti-political."

A powerful state mechanism is the greatest hindrance to any higher cultural development. Where the state has been attacked by internal decay, where the influence of political power on the creative forces of society is reduced to a minimum, there culture thrives best, for political rulership always strives for uniformity and tends to subject every aspect of social life to its guardianship. And in this it finds itself in inescapable contradiction to the creative aspirations of cultural development, which is always on the quest after new forms and fields of social activity, and for which freedom of expression, the manysidedness and the kaleidoscopic changes of things, are just as vitally necessary as rigid forms, dead rules and the forcible suppression of every manifestation of social life which are in contradiction to it.

Every culture, if its natural development is not too much affected by political restrictions, experiences a perpetual renewal of the formative urge, and out of that comes an ever growing diversity of creative activity. Every successful piece of work stirs the desire for greater perfection and deeper inspiration; each new form becomes the herald of new possibilities of development. But the state creates no culture, as is so often thoughtlessly asserted; it only tries to keep things as they are, safely anchored to stereotypes. That has been the reason for all revolutions in history.

Power operates only destructively, bent always on forcing every manifestation of life into the straitjacket of its laws. Its intellectual form of expression is dead dogma, its physical form brute force. And this unintelligence of its objectives sets its stamp on its supporters also and renders them stupid and brutal, even when they were originally endowed with the best of talents. One who is constantly striving to force everything into a mechanical order at last becomes a machine himself and loses all human feeling.

It was from the understanding of this that modern Anarchism was born and now draws its moral force. Only freedom can inspire men to great things and bring about social and political transformations. The art of ruling men has never been the art of educating men and inspiring them to a new shaping of their lives. Dreary compulsion has at its command only lifeless drill, which smothers any vital initiative at its birth and can bring forth only subjects, not free men. Freedom is the very essence of life, the impelling force in all intellectual and social development, the creator of every new outlook for the future of mankind. The liberation of man from economic exploitation and from intellectual and political oppression, which finds its finest expression in the world-philosophy of Anarchism, is the first prerequisite for the evolution of a higher social culture and a new humanity.

Chapter 2. The Proletariat and the Beginning of the Modern Labour Movement

The era of machine production and modern Capitalism; The rise of the Proletariat; The first labour unions and their struggle for existence; Luddism; Trade Unionism pure and simple; Political radicalism and labour; The Chartist movement; Socialism and the labour movement.

Modern Socialism was at first only a profounder understanding of the interconnections in social life, an attempt to solve the contradictions implicit in the present social order and to give a new content to man's relations with his social environment. Its influence was, therefore, for a time confined to a little circle of intellectuals, who for the most part came from the privileged classes. Inspired with a profound and noble sympathy for the intellectual and material needs of great masses they sought a way out of the labyrinth of social antagonisms in order to open to mankind new outlooks for its future development. For them Socialism was a cultural question; therefore, they made their appeal directly and chiefly to the reason and ethical sense of their contemporaries, hoping to find them receptive to the new insights.

But ideas do not make a movement; they are themselves merely the product of concrete situations, the intellectual precipitate of particular conditions of life. Movements arise only from the immediate and practical necessities of social life and are never the result of purely abstract ideas. But they acquire their irresistible force and their inner certainty of victory only when they are vitalised by a great idea, which gives them life and intellectual content. It is only when viewed thus that the relation of the labour movement to Socialism can be correctly understood and intelligently valued. Socialism is not the creator of the modern labour movement; rather, it grew out of it. the movement developed as the logical result of a social reconstruction out of which the present capitalist world was born. Its immediate purpose was the struggle for daily bread, the conscious resistance to a trend of things was constantly becoming more ruinous for the workers.

The modern labour movement owes its existence to the great industrial revolution which was going on in England in the latter half of the eighteenth century, and which has since then overflowed into all five continents. After the system of so-called "manufactures" had at an earlier period opened the door for a certain degree of division of labour — a division which was, however, concerned more with the methods of applying human labour than with actual technical processes — the great inventions of the subsequent period brought about a complete transformation of all the apparatus of work; the machine conquered the individual tool and created totally new forms for productive processes in general. the invention of the mechanical loom revolutionised the whole textile industry, the most important industry in England, and led to a complete new set of methods in the processing and dyeing of wool and cotton.

Through the utilisation of steam power, made available by the epoch-making invention of James Watt, machine production was freed from its dependence on the old motive forces of wind, water and horse power, and the way first properly opened for modern mass production. The use of steam made possible the operation of machines of different function in the same rooms. Thus arose the modern factory, which in a few decades had shoved the small shop to the brink of the abyss. This happened first in the textile industry; the other branches of production followed at short intervals. the utilisation of the power of steam and the invention of cast steel led in a short time to a complete revolutionising of the iron and coal industries and rapidly extended their influence to other lines of work. The development of modern big plants had as a result the fabulous growth of the industrial cities. Birmingham, which in 1801 boasted only 73,000 inhabitants, had in 1844 a population of 200,000. Sheffield in the same period grew from 46,000 to 110,000. Other centres of the new big industries grew in the same ratio.

The factories needed human fodder, and the increasingly impoverished rural population met the demand by streaming into the cities. The legislature helped, when, by the notorious *Enclosure Acts*, it robbed the small farmers of the common lands and brought them to beggary. The systematic theft of the commons had already begun under Queen Anne (1702–1714), and by 1844 had taken in more than one third of the tillable land of England and Wales. While in 1786 there had still existed 250,000 independent landowners, in the course of only thirty years their number had been reduced to 32,000.

The new machine production increased the so-called national wealth on an undreamed-of scale. But this wealth was in the hands of a small privileged minority and owed its origin to the unrestrained exploitation of the working population, which by the rapid alteration of the economic conditions of living was plunged into the most revolting misery. If one reads the dismal descriptions of the situation of the workers of that period as it is set down in the reports of the English factory inspectors, of which Marx made such effective use in his *Capital*; or if one picks up a book like Eugene Buret's *De la misère des classes labeurieuses en Angleterre et France*, to which Frederick Engels was so deeply indebted in his initial work, *The Conditions of the Working Classes in England*; or any one of numerous works by contemporary English authors, one gets a picture of that time which staggers the mind.

If Arthur Young, in his well-known account of his travels in France just before the outbreak of the Great Revolution, could declare that a large part of the French rural population stood almost on the level of beasts, having lost every trace of humanity as a result of their horrible poverty, the comparison could apply in large measure also to the intellectual and material status of the great masses of the rising industrial proletariat in the initial period of modern capitalism.

The enormous majority of the workers dwelt in miserable dirty holes without even a glass window, and they had to spend from fourteen to fifteen hours a day in the sweatshops of industry, innocent of either hygienic equipment or provision for the protection of the lives and health of the inmates. And this for a wage that was never enough to satisfy even the most indispensable of needs. If at the end of the week the worker had enough left to enable him to forget the hell he lived in for a few hours by getting drunk on bad liquor, it was the most he could achieve. The inevitable consequence of such a state of affairs was an enormous increase in prostitution, drunkenness and crime. The utter wretchedness of mankind dawns on one when he reads of the spiritual degradation and moral depravity of those masses whom no one pitied.

The pitiful situation of the factory slaves was made still more oppressive by the so-called truck system, under which the worker was compelled to purchase his provisions and other articles of daily use in the stores of the factory-owners, where often overpriced and unusable goods were handed out to him. This went so far that the worker had scarcely anything left of their hard-earned wages, and had to pay for unexpected expenses, such as doctors, medicines, and the like with the goods they had received from the factory owners, which they had, of course, to turn in in such cases at a lower price than they had been charged for them. And contemporary writers tell how mothers, in order to provide burial for a dead child, would have to pay the undertaker and the gravedigger in this way.

And this limitless exploitation of human labour-power was not confined to men and women. The new methods of work had enabled the machine to be served with just a few manual movements, which could be learned with no great difficulty. This led to the destruction of the children of the proletariat, who were put to work at the age of three or four years and had to drag out their youth in the industrial prisons of the entrepreneurs. The story of child labour, on which no restrictions of any kind were imposed at first, is one of the darkest chapters in the history of capitalism. It shows to what lengths of heartlessness a Christian management would go, untroubled by ethical considerations, and unthinkingly accustomed to unrestricted exploitation of the masses. Prolonged labour under the unwholesome conditions of the factories at last raised child mortality to the point where Richard Carlile could, with perfect justice, speak of a "gruesome repetition of the slaughter of the innocents at Bethlehem." Not until then did parliament enact laws which were for a long time evaded by the factory owners, or simply broken.

The state lent its best assistance to the freeing of management from restrictions burdensome on its lust for exploitation. It provided it with cheap labour. For this purpose, for example, there was devised the notorious Poor Law of 1834, which rouse such a storm of indignation, not only from the English working class, but from everyone who still carried a heart in his bosom. The old Poor Law, which had originated in 1601 under Queen Elizabeth, was an outcome of the suppression of the monasteries in England. The monasteries had made a practise of expending a third of their income on the maintenance of the poor. But the noble proprietors to whom the greater part of the monastic holdings had fallen had no thought of continuing to devote the required third to alms, so the law imposed on the parishes the duty of caring for the poor and finding some human means of subsistence for those whose existence had been uprooted. the law saw in poverty a personal misfortune for which the human being was not responsible, and conceded to him the right to call upon society for aid when through no fault of his own he had fallen into need and was no longer able to provide for himself. This natural consideration gave the law a social character.

The new law, however, branded poverty as crime, and laid the responsibility for personal misfortune upon alleged indolence. The new law had been brought into existence under the fateful influence of the Malthusian doctrine, whose misanthropic teachings had been hailed by the possessing classes as a new revelation. Malthus, whose well-known work on the population problem had been conceived as an answer to Godwin's *Political Justice*, had announced in blunt words that the poor man forced his way into society as an uninvited guest, and could therefore lay no claim to special rights or to the pity of his fellow men. Such a view was, of course, grist to the mill of the industrious barons and gave the required moral support to their unlimited lust for exploitation.

The new law took the provision for the maintenance of the poor out of the hands of the parish authorities and put it under a central body appointed by the state. Material support by money or provisions was for the most part abolished and replaced by the workhouse, that notorious and hated institution which in the popular speech was called the "poor law Bastille." He who, smitten by fate, was compelled to seek refuge in the workhouse, surrendered his status as a human being, for those houses were outright prisons, in which the individual was punished and humiliated for his personal misfortune. In the workhouses an iron discipline prevailed, which countered any opposition with strict punishment. Everyone had a definite task to perform; anyone who was not able to do it was deprived of food in punishment. The food was worse and more inadequate than in actual prisons, and the treatment so harsh and barbarous that children were often driven to suicide. Families were separated and their members permitted to see one another only at stated times and under the supervision of the officials. Every effort was directed to making residence in this place of terror so unendurable that only the utmost necessity would drive human beings to seek in it a last refuge. For that was the real purpose of the new poor law. Machine production had driven thousands out of their old means of living — in the textile industries alone more than 80,000 hand weavers had been made beggars by the modern big plants — and the new law saw to it that cheap labour was at the command of management, and with it the possibility of constantly forcing wages lower.

Under these horrible conditions a new social class was born, which had no forerunners in history: the modern industrial proletariat. The small craftsman of former times, who served principally the local demand, enjoyed comparatively satisfactory living conditions, which were only rarely disturbed by any considerable shock from without. He served his apprenticeship, became a journeyman, and often, later, a master himself, as the acquisition of the necessary tools of his trade was not dependent on the possession of any great amount of capital, as it became in the era of the machine. His work was worthy of a human being and still offered that natural variety which incites to creative activity and guarantees inner satisfaction to man.

Even the small home industrialist, who at the beginning of the capitalist era was already disposing of the greater part of his product to the rich lords of trade in the cities, was far from being a proletarian in the present sense. Industry, the textile industry in particular, had its centres in the rural districts, so that the small craftsmen in most instances had at his disposal a tiny bit of land, which made maintenance easier for him. And as the oncoming capitalism was before the domination of the machine, still tied to the handicraft stage of industry, its possibilities of expansion were for the time limited, since the demand for the products of industry was as a rule greater than supply, so that the worker was safeguarded against serious economic crises.

However, all that was changed within a very few years after modern machine production had began to play its part, as it was dependent in advance on mass demand, and hence on the conquest of foreign markets. Each new invention raised the capacity for production in ever increasing measure and made industrial capital the undisputed master of capitalist industry, dominating trade and finance. And since free competition, which was held by theorists to be an iron economic law, put any planned control of industrial production out of the question, at longer or shorter periods there must occur periods when, owing to various causes, the supply of industrial products outstripped the demand. This brought on abrupt cessations of production, so-called crises, which were ruinous to the proletarian population of the cities because they condemned the workers to enforced inactivity and so deprived them of the means of living. It is just this phenomenon of so-called "over production" which is so indicative of the real nature of modern capitalism — this condition in which, while factories and warehouses are crammed with wares, the actual producers are languishing in bitterest misery. It is this which reveals most plainly the horror of a system for which man is nothing and dead possessions everything.

But the developing proletariat was completely exposed to the economic fluctuations of this system, since its members had nothing to dispose of except the labour of their hands. The natural human ties which existed between the master-workman and his journeymen had no meaning for the modern proletarian. He was merely the object of exploitation by a class with which he no longer had any social relationship. For the factory owner he existed merely as a "hand," not any more as a human being. He was, one might say, the chaff which the great industrial revolution of that time had swept up in heaps in the cities, after he had lost all social standing. Socially uprooted, he had become just a component of a great mass of shipwrecked beings, who had all been smitten by the same fate. The modern proletarian, he was the man of the machine, a machine of flesh and blood who set the machine of steel in motion, to create wealth for others, while the actual producer of this wealth must perish in misery.

And dwelling close-packed with his comrades-in-misfortune in the great centres of industry not only gave a particular character to his material existence, it also gradually created for his thinking and feeling new concepts which he had not originally known. Transplanted into a new world of pounding machines and reeking chimneys, he at first merely felt himself as a wheel or a cog in a mighty mechanism against which he as an individual was helpless. He dared not even hope sooner or later to escape from this condition, since to him, as the typical dispossessed with no means of keeping alive except by the sale of his hands, every way out was barred. And not he alone, his posterity was doomed as well to the same fate. Bereft of every social tie, he was personally a mere nothing in comparison with that enormous power which was using him as the insensate tool of its selfish interests. In order to become something once more and to effect some betterment of his lot, he would have to act along with others of his kind and call a halt to the fate that had smitten him. Such considerations had sooner or later to control him if he did not wish simply to sink into the abyss; they led to the first proletarian alliances, to the modern labour movement as a whole.

It was not the "agitator" who conjured this movement of the dispossessed masses into life, as narrow-minded reactionaries and a rapacious management dared to assert then, and still assert even to-day; it was the conditions themselves which roused to life the movement and with it its spokesmen. The combination of the workers was the only means at their command for saving their lives and forcing more human conditions under which to live. The first proposals of those bands of organised wage-workers, which can be traced back to the first half of the eighteenth century, went no further than the abolition of the most crying evils of the capitalist system and some improvement of the existing conditions of living.

Since 1350 there had existed in England a statute in accordance with which apprenticeship, wages and hours were regulated by the state. The alliances of the ancient craft corporations concerned themselves only with questions relating to the production of commodities and the right of disposal of them. But when, with incipient capitalism, and the spread of "manufactures," wages began to be pushed down further and further, the first trade union organisations developed among the new class of wage-workers to combat the tendency. But these efforts of the organised workers at once encountered the unanimous resistance of the managers, who besieged the government with petitions to uphold the ancient law and suppress the "unlawful" organisations of the workers. And parliament promptly responded to this demand by passing the so-called Combination Acts of 1799–1800, which prohibited all combinations for the purpose of raising wages or improving the existing conditions of work and imposed severe penalties for violation.

Thus labour was given over unconditionally to exploitation by industrial capital, and was faced with the alternatives of, either submitting to the law and accepting without resistance all the consequences this entailed, or breaking the law which had condemned them to outright slavery. Confronted with such a choice the decision could not have been too difficult for the more courageous section of the workers, as they had scarcely more to lose anyway. They defied the law which mocked at human dignity, and tried by every means to get around its provisions. Since the trade union organisations, which were at first purely local in character and confined to particular industries, had been deprived of the legal right to exist, there sprang up all over the country so-called mutual benefit associations or similar innocuous bodies, having as their sole purpose the diverting of attention from the actual fighting organisations of the proletarians.

For the inner core of these open associations was composed of the secret conspiratory brotherhoods of the militant element among the workers, smaller or larger groups of determined men, bound by an oath to profoundest secrecy and mutual assistance. In the northern industrial sections of England and in Scotland in particular there were a large number of these secret organisations, which carried on the fight against the employers and spurred the workers to resistance. It lay in the nature of the affair that most of these struggles assumed an extremely violent character, as is easy to understand when we consider the miserable situation of the workers resulting from the disastrous development of economic conditions and the pitiless prosecutions following even the most modest attempt at improvement of the proletarian standard of living. Any violation of the letter of the law was visited with horrible punishment. Even after trade union organisations were legally recognised in 1824, the prosecutions did not cease for a long time. Conscienceless judges, openly and cynically protecting the class interests of the employers, inflicted hundreds of years imprisonment on insubordinate workers, and a considerable time elapsed before somewhat endurable conditions prevailed.

In 1812, the secret labour organisations brought about a general strike of the weavers in Glasgow. In the following years the whole of Northern England was continually shaken by strikes and unrest among the workers which finally culminated in the great strike of the spinners and weavers in Lancastershire in 1818, in which the workers, in addition to the usual demand for higher wages, called for reform of factory legislation and humane regulation of the labour of women and children. The same year brought the great strike of the Scottish miners, which was staged by their secret organisations. In the same way the greater part of the Scottish textile industry was periodically crippled by cessation of labour. Often the strikes were accompanied by arson, destruction of property and public disorder, so that the government was frequently under the necessity of throwing the militia into the industrial sections.

As later in every other country, so then in England, the resentment of the workers was directed against the introduction of the machines, the social importance of which they did not yet recognise, and which were the immediate cause of their want. As early as 1769, a special law had been enacted for the protection of the machines; but later, when the application of steam power started a rapid advance in machine production, and, in the textile industry in particular, thousands of handworkers were robbed of the means of subsistence and plunged into deepest misery, the destruction of machines became an everyday occurrence. This was the period of so-called Luddism. In 1811, over two hundred machine looms were destroyed in Nottingham. In Arnold, where the introduction of stocking-weaving machinery had thrown hundreds of the old stocking weavers on the payment, the workers stormed the factories and demolished sixty of the new machines, each of which represented an investment of forty pounds. Similar performances were repeated everywhere.

---

[1] The origin of the word is veiled in darkness. Some trace it to a weaver by the name of Ned Ludd, but there is no historical basis for this. In some regions they talked of "Jack Swing" and "Great Enoch," but the meaning of all the

What was the good of laws, so long as the need of the proletarian population was steadily increasing, and management and government had neither understanding nor sympathy for their situation! *King Ludd*[1] made his royal entry in industrial circles everywhere, and even the harshest laws were unable to put a stop to his work of destruction. "Stop him who dares; stop him who can!" was the watchword of the secret worker's societies. The destruction of the machines ceased only when a new understanding of the matter arose among themselves, and they came to see that they could not halt technical progress by this means.

In 1812, parliament enacted a law imposing the death penalty for the destruction of machines. It was on this occasion that Lord Byron delivered his celebrated indictment of the government and ironically demanded that, if the bloody law was to be put into force, the house should provide that the jury should always consist of twelve butchers.[2]

The officials put a price of forty thousand pounds in the heads of the leaders of the underground movement. In January of 1813, eighteen workers convicted of Luddism were hanged at York, and the deportation of organised workers to the penal colonies in Australia increased at a frightful rate. But the movement itself only grew the faster, particularly when the great business crisis set in after the end of the Napoleonic wars, and the discharged soldiers and sailors were added to the armies of the unemployed. This situation was made still tenser by several short harvests and the notorious corn laws of 1815, by which the price of bread was raised artificially.

But although this first phase of the modern labour movement was in great part a violent one, it still was not revolutionary in the proper sense. For this it lacked that proper understanding of the actual causes of economic and social processes which only Socialism could give it. Its violent methods were merely the result of the brutal violence which was inflicted on the workers themselves. But the methods of the young movement were not directed against the capitalist system as such at all, but merely at the abolition of its most pernicious excrescences and at the establishment of a decent human standard of living for the proletariat. "A fair days' pay for a fair day's work" was the slogan of these first unions, and when the employers resisted this modest and certainly fully justified demand of the workers with the utmost brutality, the latter were obliged to resort to whatever methods were available to them under the existing conditions.

The great historical significance of the movement lay at first less in its actual social objectives than in its simple existence. It gave a footing once more to the uprooted masses which the pressure of economic conditions had driven into the great industrial centres. It revived their social sense. The class struggle against the exploiters awakened the solidarity of the workers and gave new meaning to their lives. It breathed new hope into the victims of an economy of unrestricted exploitation and showed them a course which offered them the possibility of safeguarding their lives and defending their outraged human dignity. It strengthened the workers' self-reliance and gave them confidence in the future once more. It trained the workers in self-discipline and organised resistance, and developed in them the consciousness of their strength and their importance as a social factor in the life of their time. This was the great moral service of that movement which was born of the necessities of the situation, and which only he can undervalue who is blind to social problems and without sympathy for the sufferings of his fellow men.

---

names was the same.

[2] Lord Byron felt a strong sympathy for the Luddites, as is shown by one of his poems, the first stanza of which runs: "As the Liberty lads o'er the sea / Bought their freedom, and cheaply, with blood, / So we, boys, we / Will die fighting, or live free / And down with all kings but King Ludd!"

When, then, in 1824, the laws against the combination of workers were repealed, when the government and that section of the middle class possessed of insight had at last become convinced that even the harshest persecution would never break up the movement, the trade union organisation of the workers spread over the entire country at an undreamed-of rate. The earlier local groups combined into larger unions and thus gave to the movement its real importance. Even the reactionary turns in the government were no longer able to control this development. They merely increased the number of victims among its adherents, but they could not turn back the movement itself.

The new upsurge of political radicalism in England after the long French wars naturally had a strong influence on the English working class also. Men like Burdett, Henry Hunt, Major Cartwright, and above all William Cobbett, whose paper the *Political Register*, after the price had been reduced to twopence, attained a circulation of sixty thousand, were the intellectual heads of the new reform movement. This was directing its attacks chiefly against the corn laws, the Combination Acts of 1799–1800, and most of all, against the corrupt electoral system under which even a large part of the middle class was excluded from the franchise. Huge mass meetings in every section of the country, and particularly in the northern industrial districts, set the populace in motion. But the reactionary government under Castlereagh opposed any reform, and was determined from the first to put an end to the reform process by force. When in August, 1819, sixty thousand people poured into the Petersfield in Manchester to formulate a mass petition to the government, the assembly was dispersed by the militia, and four hundred persons were wounded or killed.

To the stormy outburst in the country against the instigators of the massacre of "Peterloo" the government replied with the notorious six gag laws, by which the right of assembly and freedom of the press were in effect suspended and the reformers made liable to the harshest prosecution. By the so-called "Cato Street Conspiracy," in which Arthur Thistlewood and his associates planned the assassination of the members of the British Cabinet, the government was given the wished for opportunity to proceed with draconic severity against the reform movement. On May 1, 1820, Thistlewood and four of his comrades paid for their attempt on the gallows: the *habeus corpus* act was suspended for two years, and England was delivered to a reactionary regime which respected none of the rights of its citizens.

This put a stop to the movement for the time being. Then the July revolution of 1830 in France led to a revival of the English reform movement, which, this time, took on an entirely different character. The fight for parliamentary reform flared up anew. But after the bourgeoisie saw the greater part of their demands satisfied by the Reform Bill of 1832, a victory which they owned only to the energetic support of the workers, they opposed all further attempts at reform, looking towards universal suffrage, and left the workers to depart empty-handed. Not only that: the new parliament enacted a number of reactionary laws by which the workers' right to organise was again seriously threatened. The shining examples among these new laws were the notorious poor laws of 1834, to which reference has already been made. The workers felt that they had been sold and betrayed, and this feeling led to a complete break with the middle class.

The new reform movement from now on found vigorous expression in the developing Chartism, which, it is true, was supported by a considerable part of the petty-bourgeoisie, but in which the proletarian element everywhere took and energetic part. Chartism, of course, had inscribed on its banner the celebrated six points of the charter, which aimed at radical parliamentary reform, but it had also appropriated all the social demands of the workers and was trying by every form of direct attack to transform these into realities. Thus J.R. Stevens, one of the most influential leaders of the Chartist movement, declared before a great mass meeting in Manchester that Chartism was not a political question which would be settled by the introduction of universal suffrage, but was instead to be regarded as a "bread and butter question," since the charter would mean good homes, abundant food, human associations and short hours of labour for the workers. It was for this reason that propaganda for the celebrated Ten-Hour Bill played such an important part in the movement.

With the Chartist movement England had entered upon a revolutionary period, and wide circles of both the bourgeoisie and the working class were convinced that a civil war was close at hand. Huge mass meetings in every section of the country testified to the rapid spread of the movement, and numerous strikes and constant unrest in the cities gave it a threatening aspect. The frightened employers organised numerous armed leagues "for the protection of persons and property" in the industrial centres. This led to the workers also beginning to arm. By a resolution of the Chartist convention, which convened in London in March of 1839, and was later moved to Birmingham, fifteen of their best orators were sent out to every section of the country to make the people aquatinted with the aims of the movement and to collect signatures to the Chartist petition. Their meetings were attended by hundreds of thousands, and showed what a response the movement had aroused among the masses of the people.

Chartism had a large number of intelligent and self-sacrificing spokesmen (such as William Lovell, Feargus O'Connor, Branterre O'Brien, J.R. Stephens, Henry Hetherington, James Watson, Henry Vincent, John Taylor, A.H. Beaumont, Ernest Jones, to mention only a few of the best known.) It commanded, in addition, a fairly widespread press, of which papers like *The Poor Man's Guardian* and the *Northern Star* exerted the greatest influence. Chartism was, as a matter of fact, not a movement with definite aims, but rather a catchbasin for the social discontent of the time, but it did effect a shaking-up, especially of the working class, whom it made receptive to far-reaching social aims. Socialism also forged vigorously ahead during the Chartist period, and the ideas of William Thompson, John Gray, and especially of Robert Owen, began to spread more widely among the English workers.

In France, Belgium and the Rhine country also, where industrial capitalism first established itself on the Continent, it was everywhere accompanied by the same phenomena and led, of necessity, to the initial stages of a labour movement. And this movement manifested itself at first in every country in the same primitive form, which only gradually yielded to a better understanding, until at last its permeation by Socialist ideas endowed it with loftier conceptions and opened for it new social outlooks. The alliance of the labour movement with Socialism was of decisive importance for both. But the political ideas which influenced this, that or the other Socialist school determined the character of the movement in each instance, and its outlook for the future as well.

While certain schools of Socialism remained quite indifferent or unsympathetic to the young labour movement, others of them realised the real importance of this movement as the necessary preliminary to the realisation of Socialism. They understood that it must be their task to take an active part in the everyday struggles of the workers, so as to make clear to the toiling masses the intimate connection between their immediate demands and the Socialist objectives. For these struggles, growing out of the needs of the moment, serve to bring about a correct understanding of the profound importance of the liberation of the proletariat for the complete suppression of wage slavery. Although sprung from the immediate necessities of life, the movement, nevertheless, bore within it the germ of things to come, and these were to set new goals for life. Everything new arises from the realities of vital being. New worlds are not born in the vacuum of abstract ideas, but in the fight for daily bread in that hard and ceaseless struggle which the needs and worries of the hour demand just to take care of the indispensable requirements of life. In the constant warfare against the already existing, the new shapes itself and comes to fruition. He who does not know how to value the achievements of the hour will never be able to conquer a better future for himself and his fellows.

From the daily battles against the employers and their allies, the workers gradually learn the deeper meaning of this struggle. At first they pursue only the immediate purpose of improving the status of the producers within the existing social order, but gradually they lay bare the root of the evil — monopoly economy and its political and social accompaniments. For the attainment of such an understanding the everyday struggles are better educative material than the finest theoretical discussions. Nothing can so impress the mind and soul of the worker as this enduring battle for daily bread, nothing makes him so receptive to the teachings of Socialism as the incessant struggle for the necessities of life.

Just as in the time of feudal domination the bondmen peasants by their frequent uprisings — which had at first only the purpose of wresting from the feudal lords certain concessions which would mean some betterment of their dreary standard of living — prepared the way for the Great Revolution by which the abolition of feudal privileges was practically brought about; so the innumerable labour was within capitalist society constitute, one might say, the introduction to that great social revolution of the future which shall make Socialism a living reality. Without the incessant revolts of the peasantry — Taine reports that between 1781 and the storming of the Bastille nearly five hundred of these revolts occurred in almost every part of France — the idea of the perniciousness of the whole system of serfdom and feudalism would never have entered the heads of the masses.

That is just how it stands with the economic and social struggles of the modern working class. It would be utterly wrong to estimate these merely on the basis of their material origin or their practical results and to overlook their deeper psychological significance. Only from the everyday conflicts between labour and capital could the doctrines of Socialism, which had arisen in the minds of individual thinkers, take on flesh and blood and aquire that peculiar character which make of them a mass movement, the embodiment of a new cultural ideal for the future.

Chapter 3. The Forerunners of Syndicalism

Robert Owen and the English labour movement; The Grand National Consolidated Trade Union; William Benbow and the idea of the General Strike; The period of reaction; Evolution of the labour organisations in France; The International Workingmen's Association; The new conception of trade unionism; The idea of the labour councils; Labour councils versus dictatorships; Bakunin on the economic organisation of the workers; The introduction of parliamentary politics by Marx and Engels and the end of the International.

The permeation of the labour movement by Socialist ideas early led to tendencies which had an unmistakable relationship to the revolutionary syndicalism of our day. These tendencies developed first in England, the mother country of capitalist big industry, and for a time strongly influenced the advanced sections of the English working class. After the repeal of the Combination Acts, the effort of the workers was directed chiefly to giving a broader character to their trade union organisations, as practical experience had shown them that purely local organisations could not provide the needed support in their struggles for daily bread. Still these efforts were not at first based on any very profound social concepts. The workers, insofar as they were influenced by the political reform movement of that time, had no goal whatever in view outside the immediate betterment of their economic status. Not until the beginning of the 30's did the influence of Socialist ideas on the English labour movement become plainly apparent, and its appearance then is to be ascribed chiefly to the stirring propaganda of Robert Owen and his followers.

A few years before the convening of the so-called Reform Parliament the *National Union of the Working Classes* was founded, its most important component part being the workers in the textile industries. This combination had summed up its demands in the following four points:

1. To every worker the full value of his labour.

2. Protection of the worker against the employers by every appropriate means, which means will develop automatically out of the current conditions.

3. The reform of parliament and universal suffrage for both men and women.

4. Education of workers in economic problems. One recognises in these demands the strong influence of the political reform movement which just at that time held the entire country under its spell: but at the same time one notices expressions which are borrowed from the doctrines of Robert Owen.

The year 1832 brought the Reform Bill, by which the last political illusions for large circles of the English working class were destroyed. When the bill had become law it was seen that the middle class had, indeed, won a great victory over the aristocratic landowners, but the workers recognised that they had been betrayed again, and that they had merely been used by the bourgeoisie to pull its chestnuts out of the fire. The result was a general disillusionment and the steadily sprawling conviction that the working class could find no help in an alliance with the bourgeoisie. If, before then, the class struggle had been an actuality which rose spontaneously out of the conflicting economic interests of the possessing and non-possessing classes, it had now taken shape as a definite conviction in the minds of the workers and gave a determinate course to their activities. This turn in the thinking of the working class is clearly revealed in numerous utterances in labour press during those years. The workers were beginning to understand that their real strength lay in their character as producers. The more keenly aware they became of the fiasco of their participation in the political reform movement, the more firmly rooted became their newly acquired understanding of their own economic importance in society.

They were strengthened in this conviction in high degree by the propaganda of Robert Owen, who at that time was gaining constantly stronger influence in the ranks of organised labour. Owen recognised that the steady growth of trade union organisations furnished a firm basis for his efforts at a fundamental alteration of the capitalist economic order, and this filled him with high hopes. He showed the workers that the existing conflict between capital and labour could never be settled by ordinary battles over wages, though, in fact, he by no means overlooked the great importance of these to the workers. On the other hand he strove to convince the workers that they could expect nothing whatever from legislative bodies, and must take their affairs into their own hands. These ideas found willing ears among the advanced sectors of the English working class, and first manifested themselves strongly among the building trades. The *Builders' Union*, in which were combined a considerable number of local labour unions, was at that time one of the most advanced and most active of labour organisations, and was a thorn in the flesh of the managers. In the year 1831, Owen had presented his plans for the reconstruction of society before a meeting of delegates of this union in Manchester. The plans amounted to a kind of Guild Socialism and called for the establishment of producer's co-operatives under the control of the trade unions. The proposals were adopted, and shortly after this the Builders' Union was involved in a long serious of severe conflicts, the unhappy outcome of which seriously threatened the existence of the organisation and put a premature end to all efforts in the direction marked out by Owen.

Owen did not let himself be discouraged by this, but carried on his activities with renewed zeal. In 1833 there convened in London a conference of trade unions and co-operative organisations, at which Owen explained exhaustively his plan for social reconstruction by the workers themselves. From the reports of the delegates one can see plainly what an influence these ideas has already gained and what a creative spirit then animated the advanced circles of the English working class. *The Poor Man's Guardian* very justly summed up its report of the conference in these words:

> "But far different from the paltry objects of all former combinations is that now aimed at by the congress of delegates. Their reports show that an entire change in society — a change amounting to a complete subversion of the existing order of the world — is contemplated by the working classes. They aspire to be at the top instead of the bottom of society — or rather that there should be no bottom or top at all."

The immediate result of this conference was the founding of the *Grand National Consolidated Trade Union of Great Britain and Ireland* at the beginning of 1834. These were stirring times. The whole country was shaken by innumerable strikes and lock-outs, and the number of workers organised in trade unions rapidly soared to 800,000. The founding of the G.N.C. arose from the effort to gather the scattered organisations into one great federation, which would give greater effective force to the actions of the workers. But what distinguished this alliance from all the efforts in this direction which had been made previously was that it stood, neither for pure trade unionism, not for collaboration of the workers with the political reformers. The G.N.C. was conceived as a fighting organisation to lend all possible aid to the needed betterment of their condition, but it had at the same time set itself the goal of overthrowing capitalist economy as a whole and replacing it with the co-operative labour of all producers, which should no longer have in view profits for all individuals, but the satisfaction of the needs of all. The G.N.C. was, then, to be the framework within which these aspirations would find expression and be transformed into reality.

The organisers wanted to combine in these federations the workers in all industrial and agricultural pursuits and group them according to their special branches of production. Each industry would constitute a special division which would concern itself with the special conditions of their productive activity and the related administrative functions. Wherever this was possible the workers in the various branches were to proceed to the establishment of co-operative plants, which should sell their produce to consumers at actual cost, including the expense of administration. Universal organisation would serve to bind the separate industries together organically, and to regulate their mutual interests. The exchange of products of the co-operative plants was to be effected through so-called labour bazaars and the use of special exchange-money or labour tickets. By the steady spread of these institutions they hoped to drive capitalist competition from the field and thus to achieve a complete reorganisation of society.

At the same time these co-operative agricultural and industrial undertakings were to serve to make the day-to-day struggles of the workers in the capitalist world easier. This is shown particularly in three of the seven points in which the G.N.C. had framed its demands:

> "As land is the source of the first necessaries of life, and as, without the possession of it, the producing classes will ever remain in a greater or less degree subservient to the money capitalists, and subsequent upon the fluctuations of trade and commerce, this committee advises that a great effort should be made by the unions to secure such portions of it on lease as their funds will permit, in order that in all turn-outs the men may be employed in rearing the greater part, if not the whole, of their subsistence under the direction of practical agricultural superintendents, which arrangements would not have the effect of lowering the price of labour in any trade, but on the contrary would rather tend to increase it by drawing off the at present superfluous supply in manufactures.
>
> "The committees would, nevertheless, earnestly recommend in all cases of strikes and turn-outs, where it is practicable, that the men be employed in the making or producing of commodities as would be in demand among their brother unionists; and that to effect this, each lodge should be provided with a workroom or shop in which these commodities may be manufactured on account of such lodge, which shall make proper arrangements for the supply of the necessary materials.
>
> "That in all cases where it is practicable, each district or branch should establish one or more depots of provisions and articles in general domestic use: by which

means the working man may be supplied with the bast commodities at little above wholesale prices."

The G.N.C. was, therefore, conceived by its founders as an alliance of trade unions and co-operatives. By his practical participation in co-operative undertakings the worker was to gain the understanding necessary for the administration of the industry and thus be fitted to bring ever wider circles of social production under their control, until at last the whole economic life should be conducted by the producers themselves and an end put to all exploitation. These ideas found surprisingly clear expression in worker's meetings and, more particularly, in the labour press. If, for example, one reads *The Pioneer*, the organ of the G.N.C. managed by James Morrison, one frequently encounters arguments that sound thoroughly modern. This is revealed especially in the discussions with the political reformers, who had inscribed on their banner the democratic reconstruction of the House of Commons. They were told in reply that the workers had no interest whatever in efforts of that sort, since an economic transformation of society in the Socialist sense would render the House of Commons superfluous. Its place would be taken by the labour boards and the industrial federations, which would concern themselves with merely with the problems of production and consumption in the interest of the people. These organisations were destined to take over the functions of the present entrepreneurs; with common ownership of all social wealth there would no longer be any need for political institutions. The wealth of the nation would no longer be determined by the quantity of goods produced, but by the personal advantage that every individual derived from them. The House of Commons would in the future be merely a *House of Trades*.

The G.N.C. met with an extraordinary response from the workers. In a few months it embraced much over half a million members, and even though its actual aims were clearly understood at first only by the most intellectually active elements among the workers, still the great masses recognised, at least, that an organisation of such dimensions could lend much greater weight to their demands than could local groups. The agitation for the ten-hour day had then taken firm hold on all sections of the English working class, and the G.N.C. set itself with all its energy to enforce this demand. Owen himself, and his close friends Doherty, Fielden and Grant took a prominent part in this movement. However, the militants in the G.N.C. placed little hope in legislation, but tried to convince the workers that the ten-hour day could only be won by the united economic action of the whole body of workers. "The adults in factories must by unions among themselves make a *Short Time Bill* for themselves." This was their slogan.

The idea of the general strike met with undivided sympathy from the organised English workers. At the beginning of 1832, William Benbow, one of the most active champions of the new movement, had published a pamphlet entitled *Grand National Holiday and Congress of the Productive Classes*, which had a tremendous circulation, and in which the idea of the general strike and its importance to the working class was for the first time treated in its full compass. Benbow told the workers that if the enforced sale of their labour power was the cause of their slavery, then their organised refusal to work must be the means of their liberation. Such an instrument of warfare dispensed with any use of physical force and could achieve incomparably greater effects that the best army. All that was needed to bring about the downfall of the system of organised injustice was that the workers should grasp the importance of this powerful weapon and learn to use it with intelligence. Benbow advance a lot of proposals, such as preparation for the general strike in the whole country by the establishment of local committees, so that the eruption might burst with elemental force, and his ideas at that time met with the heartiest response from the workers.

The rapid growth of the G.N.C. and, even more, the spirit that emanated from it, filled the employers with secret fear and blind hatred of the new combination. They felt that the movement must be stifled at the very outset before it had time to be spread farther and build up and consolidate its local groups. The entire bourgeois press denounced the "criminal purposes" of the G.N.C., and unanimously proclaimed that it was leading the country toward a catastrophe. The factory owners in every industry besieged parliament with petitions urging measures against "unlawful combinations," and in particular against the collaboration of workers in different categories in industrial disputes. Many employers laid before their workers the so-called "document," and offered them the alternative of withdrawing from their unions or being thrown on the street by a lock-out.

Parliament did not, it is true, re-enact the old Combination Acts, but the government encouraged the judges to deal with the "excesses" of the workers as severely as they could within the framework of the existing laws. And they did so in generous measure, being often able to use as a handle the fact that many unions had retained from the days of their underground activity before the repeal of the Combination Acts the formula of the oath and other ceremonial forms, and that this was contrary to the letter of the law. hundreds of workers were sentenced to horrible punishments for the most trivial offences. Among the terrorist sentences of that time that imposed on six field hands in Dorchester aroused the bitterest indignation. Through the initiative of the G.N.C. the field workers in Tolpuddle, a little village near Dorchester, had formed a union and demanded an increase of wages from seven shillings to eight shillings a week. Shortly afterward six field hands were arrested and sentenced to the frightful penalty of transportation for seven years to the penal colonies in Australia. Their sole crime consisted in belonging to a union.

Thus from the very beginning the G.N.C. was involved in a long series of important wage wars and was subjected besides to constant and bitter prosecutions, so that it hardly found time to begin in earnest its great work of educating the masses. Perhaps, in any case, the time for that was not yet ripe. Many of its members turned to the awakening Chartism, which accepted many of its immediate demands, and along with other matters kept up the propaganda for the general strike, culminating in 1842 in that great movement which tied up all the industries of Lancashire, Yorkshire, Staffordshire, the Potteries, Wales and the coal districts of Scotland. But the original significance of the movement had worn off, and Owen had been right when he accused Chartism of laying too much weight of political reform and showing too little understanding of the great economic problems. The unhappy revolutions of 1848–49 on the continent led also to the decline of the Chartist movement, and pure trade unionism came once more to dominate the field for years in the English labour movement.

In France also the alliance of Socialism with the labour movement quickly led to attempts on the part of the workers to overthrow the capitalist economic order and pave the way for a new social development. The antagonism between the working class and the bourgeoisie that had just acquired mastery had already shown itself clearly during the storms of the Great Revolution. Before the Revolution the workers had been united in the so-called *Compagnonnages*, whose origin can be traced back to the fifteenth century. These were associations of journeymen craftsmen which had their particular ceremonials transmitted from the middle ages, whose members were pledges to mutual assistance, and which busied themselves with the concerns of their calling, but also resorted often to strikes and boycotts to protect their immediate economic interests. With the abolition of the guilds and the development of modern industry these bodies gradually lost their importance and gave way to new forms of proletarian organisation.

By the law of August 21, 1790, all citizens were conceded the right of free combination within the framework of the existing laws, and the workers availed themselves of this right by organising themselves in trade unions for the safeguarding of their interests against the employers. A lot of local strike movements ensued, especially in the building industry, and caused the employers a great deal of worry, as the organisations of workers grew constantly stronger, counting 80,000 members in Paris alone.

In a memorial to the government the employers denounced these combinations of workers and demanded the protection of the state against this "new tyranny" which presumed to interfere with the right of free contract between employer and employee. The government responded graciously to this demand and forbade all combinations for the purpose of effecting alterations in the existing conditions of labour, assigning as a reason that it could not permit the existence of a state within the state. This prohibition continued in force until 1864. But here also it was early shown that circumstances are stronger than the law. Just as had the English, so also the French workers resorted to secret association, since the law denied them the right to urge their demands openly.

The so-called *mutualités*, harmless mutual benefit societies, often served in this connection as a cover, spreading the mantle of legality as over the secret organisations for resistance (*sociétés de resistance*). These had, it is true, often to endure harsh prosecutions, and to make many sacrifices, but no law was able to crush their resistance. Under the law of Louis Phillipe the laws against the combination of workers were strengthened still further, but even that could not prevent the steady growth of the *sociétés de resistance*, nor the development of a long series of great strike movements as a result of their underground activities. Of these the fight of the weavers in Lyons in 1831 grew into an event of European importance. Bitter need had spurred these workers to a desperate resistance to the rapacity of the employers, and owing to the interference of the militia this had developed into an outright revolt, into which the workers carried their banner inscribed with the significant words: "Live working or die fighting!"

As early as the 30's a lot of these workers' associations had become acquainted with Socialist ideas, and after the February Revolution of 1848 the acquaintance afforded the basis for the movement of the French *Workingmens' Association*, a co-operative movement with a trade union trend, which worked for a reshaping of society by constructive effort. In his history of the movement S. Englander puts the number of these associations at about two thousand. But *the coup d'état* of Louis Bonaparte put an abrupt end to this hopeful beginning, as to so many others.

Only with the founding of the *International Workingmen's Association* was there a revival of the doctrines of a militant and constructive Socialism, but after that they spread internationally. The International, which exercise such a powerful influence on the intellectual development of the body of European workers, and which even today has not lost its magnetic attraction in the Latin countries, was brought into being by the collaboration of the English and French workers in 1864. It was the first great attempt to unite the workers of all countries in an international alliance which should open the path for the social and economic liberation of the working class. It was from the beginning distinguished from all the political forms of organisation of bourgeois radicalism by pointing out that the economic subservience of the workers to the owners of the raw materials and the tools of production was the source of the slavery which revealed itself in social misery, intellectual degradation, and political oppression. For this reason it proclaimed in its statutes the economic liberation of the working class as the great purpose to which every political movement must be subordinate.

Since the most important object was to unite the different factions of the social movement in Europe for this purpose, the organisational structure of the vast workers' alliance was based on the principles of Federalism, which guaranteed to each particular school the possibility of working for this common goal in accordance with their own convictions and on the basis of the particular conditions of each country. The International did not stand for any defined social system; it was rather the expression of a movement whose theoretical principles slowly matured in the practical struggles of everyday life and took clearer form at every stage of its vigorous growth. the first need was to bring the workers of the different countries closer to one another, to make them understand that their economic and social enslavement was everywhere traceable to the same causes, and that consequently the manifestation of their solidarity must reach beyond the artificial boundaries of the states, since it is not tied up with the alleged interests of the nation, but with the lot of their class.

The practical efforts of its sections to end the importation of foreign strike-breakers in times of industrial warfare, and to furnish material and moral assistance to militant workers in every country by international collections, contributed more to the development of an international consciousness among the workers than the loveliest theories could have done. They gave the workers practical education in social philosophy. It was a fact that after every considerable strike the membership of the International soared mightily, and the conviction of its national coherence and homogeneity was constantly strengthened.

Thus the International became the great school mistress of the socialist labour movement and confronted the capitalist world with the world of international labour, which was being ever more firmly welded together in the bonds of proletarian solidarity. The first two congresses of the International, at Geneva in 1866, and at Lausanne in 1867, were characterised by a spirit of comparative moderation. They were the first tentative efforts of a movement which was only slowly becoming clear as to its task, and was seeking for a definite expression. But the great strike movements in France, Belgium, Switzerland and other countries gave the International a powerful forward impetus and revolutionised the minds of the workers, a change to which the powerful revival during that period of the democratic ideas, which had suffered a severe setback after the collapse of the revolutions of 1848–49, contributed not a little.

The congress at Brussels, in 1868, was animated by a totally different spirit from that of its two predecessors. It was felt that the workers everywhere were awakening to new life and were becoming constantly surer of the subject of their endeavours. The congress, by a large majority, declared itself for the collectivising of the land and other means of production, and called upon the sections in the different countries to go exhaustively into this question, so that at the next congress a clear decision could be reached. With this the international took on an outspokenly Socialistic character, which was most happily complemented by the outstandingly libertarian tendency of the workers in the Latin countries. The resolution to prepare the workers for a general strike to meet the danger of a threatened war, because they were the only class that could by energetic intervention prevent the organised mass murder, also testified to the spirit by which the International was permeated at that time.

At the congress in Basel in 1869 the ideational development of the great workers' alliance reached its zenith. The congress concerned itself only with questions which had an immediate concern with the economic and social problems of the working class. It ratified the resolutions which the Brussels congress had adopted concerning the collective ownership of the means of production, leaving the question of the organisation of labour open. But the interesting debates at the Basel congress show very plainly that the advanced sections of the International had already been giving attention to this question, and had, moreover, come to very clear conclusions about it. The was revealed particularly in the utterances concerning the importance of trade union organisations of the working class. In the report upon the question which Eugène Hins laid before the congress in the name of the Belgian Federation there was presented for the first time a wholly new point of view, which had an unmistakable resemblance to certain ideas of Owen and the English labour movement of the 30's.

In order to make a correct estimate of this one must remember that the various schools of state-socialism of that time attributed to the trade unions either no importance at all or at best only a subordinate one. The French Blanquists saw in the trade unions merely a reform movement, with which they wished to have nothing to do, as their immediate aim was a socialist dictatorship. Ferdinand Lassalle directed all his activities toward wielding the workers into a political party and was an outspoken opponent of all trade union endeavours, in which he saw only a hindrance to the political evolution of the working class. Marx, and more especially his friends of that period in Germany, recognised, it is true, the necessity of the trade unions for the achievement of certain betterments within the capitalist social system, but they believed that their role would be exhausted with this, and that they would disappear along with capitalism, since the transition to Socialism could be guided only by a proletarian dictatorship.

At Basel this idea underwent for the first time a thorough critical examination. In the Belgian report Hins laid before the Congress, the views expressed in which were expressed by the delegates from Spain, the Swiss Jura, and a considerable part of the French sections, it was clearly set forth that the trade union organisations of the workers not only had a right to existence within the present society, but they were even more to be regarded as the social cells of a coming Socialist order, and it was, therefore, the task of the International to educate them for this service. In accordance with this the congress adopted the following resolution:

> "The Congress declares that all workers should strive to establish associations for resistance in their various trades. As soon as a trade union is formed the unions on the same trade are to be notified so that the formation of national alliances in the industries may be begun. These alliances shall be charged with the duty of collecting all material relating to their industry, of advising about measures to be executed in common, and of seeing that they are carried out, to the end, that the present wage system be replaced by the federation of free producers. The Congress directs the General Council to provide for the alliance of the trade unions of all countries."

In his argument for the resolution proposed by the committee Hins explained that "by this double form of organisation of local workers' associations and general alliances for each industry on the one hand the political administration of the committees, and on the other, the general representation of labour, regional, national and international will be provided for. *The councils of the trade and industrial organisations will take the place of the present government, and this representation of labour will do away, once and forever, with the governments of the past.*"

This new and fruitful idea grew out of the recognition that every new economic form must be accompanied by a new political form of the social organism and could only attain political expression in this. Therefore, Socialism also had to have a special political form of expression, within which it may become a living thing, and they thought they had found this form in *a system of labour councils*. The workers in the Latin countries, in which the International found its principal support, developed their movement on the basis of economic fighting organisations and Socialist propaganda groups, and worked in the spirit of the Basel resolutions.

As they recognised in the state the political agent and defender of the possessing classes, they did not strive at all for the conquest of political power, but for the overthrow of the state and of every form of political power, in which with sure instinct they saw the requisite preliminary conditions for all tyranny and all exploitation. They did, therefore, not choose to imitate the bourgeois classes and set up a political party, thus preparing the way for a new class of professional politicians, whose goal was the conquest of the political power. They understood that, along with the monopoly of property, the monopoly of power must also be destroyed if complete reshaping of social life was to be achieved. Proceeding from their recognition that the lordship of man over man had had its day, they sought to familiarise themselves with the administration of things. So to the state politics of the parties they opposed the economic policy of the workers. They understood that the reorganisation of society on a Socialist pattern must be carried out in the various branches of industry and in the departments of agrarian production; of this understanding was born the idea of a system of labour councils.

It was this same idea which inspired large sections of the Russian workers and peasants at the outbreak of the revolution, even if the idea had never been thought out so clearly and systematically in Russia as in the sections of the First International. Under tsarism the Russian workers lacked the requisite intellectual preparation for this. But Bolshevism put an abrupt end to this fruitful idea. For the despotism of dictatorship stands in irreconcilable contradiction to the constructive idea of the council system, that is, to a Socialist reconstruction of society by the producers themselves. The attempt to combine the two by force could only lead to that soulless bureaucracy which has been so disastrous for the Russian Revolution. The council system brooks no dictatorships as it proceeds from totally different assumptions. In it is embodied the will from below, the creative energy of the toiling masses. In dictatorship, however, only lives barren compulsion from above, which will suffer no creative activity and proclaims blind submission as the highest laws for all. The two cannot exist together. In Russia dictatorship proved victorious. Hence there are no more soviets there. All that is left of them is the name and a gruesome caricature of its original meaning.

The council system for labour embraces large part of the economic forms employed by a constructive Socialism which of its own accord operates and produces to meet all natural requirements. It was the direct result of a fruitful development of ideas growing out of the Socialist labour movement. This particular idea rose from the effort to provide a concrete basis for the realisation of Socialism. This basis was seen to lie in the constructive employment of every efficient human being. But dictatorship in an inheritance from bourgeois society, the traditional precipitate of French Jacobinism which was dragged into the proletarian movement by the so-called Babouvists and later taken over by Marx and his followers. The idea of the council system is intimately intergrown with Socialism and is unthinkable without it; dictatorship, however, has nothing whatever in common with Socialism, and at best can only lead to the most barren of state capitalism.

Dictatorship is a definite form of state power: the state in state of siege. Like all other advocates of the state idea, so also the advocates of dictatorship proceed from the assumption that any alleged advance and every temporal necessity must be forced on the people from above. This assumption alone makes dictatorship the greatest obstacle to any social revolution, the proper element of which is the free initiative and constructive activity of the people. Dictatorship is the negation of organic development, of natural building from below upwards, it is the proclamation of the wardship of the toiling people, a guardianship forced upon the masses by a tiny minority. *Even if its supporters are animated by the very best intentions*, the iron logic of the facts will always drive them into the camp of extremest despotism. Russia had given us the most instructive example of this. And the pretence that the so-called *dictatorship of the proletariat* is something different, because we have here to do with the dictatorship of a class, not the dictatorship of individuals, deceives no earnest critic; it is only a sophisticated trick to fool simpletons. Such a thing as the dictatorship of a class is utterly unthinkable, since there will always be involved merely the dictatorship of a particular party which takes upon itself to speak *in the name of a class*, just as the bourgeoisie justified any despotic proceeding *in the name of a people*.

The idea of a council system for labour was the practical overthrow of the state idea as a whole; it stands, therefore, in frank antagonism to any form of dictatorship, which must always have in view the highest development the power of the state. The pioneers of this idea in the First International recognised that economic equality without social and political liberty is unthinkable; for this reason they were firmly convinced that the liquidation of all institutions of political power must be the first task of the social revolution, so as to make any new form of exploitation impossible. They believed that the workers' International was destined gradually to gather all effective workers into its ranks, and at the proper time to overthrow the economic despotism of the possessing classes, and along with this all the political coercive institutions of the capitalist state, and to replace these by a new order of things. This conviction was held by all libertarian sections of the international. Bakunin expressed it in the following words:

> "Sine the organisation of the International has as its goal, not the setting up of new states or despots, but the radical destruction of every separate sovereignty, it must have an essentially different character from the organisation of the state. To just the degree that the latter is authoritarian, artificial and violent, alien and hostile to the natural development and the interests of the people, to that same degree must the International be free, natural and in every respect in accord with these interests and instincts. But what is the natural organisation of the masses? It is one based on the different occupations of their actual daily life, on their various kinds of work, organisations according to their occupations, trade organisations. When all industries, including the various branches of agriculture, are represented in the International, its organisation, the organisation of the masses of the people, will be finished."

From this line of thought arose likewise the idea of opposing to the bourgeois parliaments a *Chamber of Labour*, which proceeded from the ranks of the Belgian Internationalists. Theses labour chambers were to represent the organised labour of every trade and Industry, and were to concern themselves with all questions of social economy and economic organisation on a Socialist basis, in order to prepare practically for the taking over by the organised workers of the means of production, and in this spirit to provide for the intellectual training of the producers. In addition these bodies were to pass judgement from the workers' point of view on all questions brought up in the bourgeois parliaments which were of interest to the workers, so as to contrast the policies of bourgeois society with the views of the workers. Max Nettlau has given to the public in his book *Der Anarchismus von Proudhon zu Kropotkin*, a hitherto unknown passage from one of Bakunin's manuscripts that is highly indicative of Bakunin's views on this question:

> "...All this practical and vital study of social science by the workers themselves in their trade sections and in these chambers will, and already has, engendered in them the unanimous, well-considered, theoretically and practically demonstrable conviction that the *serious, final, complete liberation of the workers is possible only upon one condition, that of the appropriation of capital, that is, of raw material and all the tools of labour, including land by the whole body of workers.* ...The organisation of the trade sections, their federation in the International, and their representation by the Chambers of Labour, not only create a great academy, in which the workers of the International, combining theory and practice, can and must study economic science, they also bear in themselves the living germs of *the new social order,* which is to replace the bourgeois world. They are creating not only the ideas but also the facts of the future itself"

These ideas were at that time generally disseminated in the sections of the International in Belgium, Holland, the Swiss Jura, France and Spain, and gave to the Socialism of the great workers' alliance a peculiar social character, which with the development of political labour parties in Europe was for a considerable time almost completely forgotten, and only in Spain never exhausted its power to win converts, as recent events in that country have so clearly shown. They found active advocates in men like James Guillaume, Adhémar Schwitzguébel, Eugène Varlin, Louis Pindy, César De Paepe, Eugène Hins, Hector Denis, Guillaume De Greef, Victor Arnould, R. Farga Pellicer, G. Sentiñon, Anselmo Lorenzo, to mention here only the best-known names, all men of excellent reputation in the International. The fact is that the whole intellectual development of the International is to be ascribed to the enthusiasm of these libertarian elements in it, and received no stimulus from either the state Socialist factions in Germany and Switzerland or pure Trades Unionism in England.

So long as the International pursued these general lines, and for the best respected the right of decision of the separate federations, as was provided in its statutes, it exercised an irresistible influence over the organised workers. But that changed at once when Marx and Engels began to use their position in the London General Council to commit the separate national federations to parliamentary action. This occurred first at the unhappy London Conference of 1871. This behaviour was in sharp violation not only of the spirit but also of the statutes of the International. It could but encounter the united resistance of all the libertarian elements in the International, the more so as the question had never previously been brought before a congress for consideration.

Shortly after the London Conference the Jura Federation published the historic circular on Sonvillier, which protested in determined and unequivocal words against the arrogant presumption of the London General Council. But the congress at The Hague in 1872, in which a majority had been artificially created by the employment of the dirtiest and most reprehensible methods, crowned the work begun by the London Conference of transforming the International into an electoral machine. In order to obviate any misunderstanding the Blanquist, Edwouard Vaillant, in his argument for the resolution proposed by the General Council advocating the conquest of political power by the working class, explained that "as soon as this resolution has been adopted by the Congress and so incorporated into the Bible of the International, it will be the duty of every member to follow it under penalty of expulsion." By this Marx and his followers directly provoked the open split in the International with all its disastrous consequences for the development of the labour movement, and inaugurated the period of parliamentary politics which of natural necessity led to that intellectual stagnation and moral degeneration of the Socialist movement which we can observe today in most countries.

Soon after the Hague Congress the delegates of the most important energetic federations of the International met in the anti-authoritarian congress in St. Immier, which declared all the resolutions adopted at the Hague null and void. From then on dates the split in the Socialist camp between the advocates of direct revolutionary action and the spokesmen for parliamentary politics, which with the lapse of time has grown constantly wider and more unbridgeable. Marx and Bakunin were merely the most prominent representatives of the opposed factions in this struggle between two different conceptions of the fundamental principles of Socialism. But it would be a big mistake to try to explain this struggle as merely a conflict between two personalities; it was the antagonism between two sets of ideas which gave to this struggle its real importance and still gives it today. That Marx and Engels gave such a spiteful and personal character to the dissension was a disaster. The International had room for every faction, and a continuous discussion of the different views could only have contributed to their clarification. But the effort to make all schools of thought subservient to one particular school, one which, moreover, represented only a minority in the International, could but lead to a cleavage and to the decline of the great alliance of workers, could but destroy those promising germs which were of such great importance to the labour movement in every land.

The Franco-Prussian War, by which the focal point of the Socialist movement was transferred to Germany, whose workers had neither revolutionary traditions not that rich experience possessed by Socialists in the countries to the west, contributed greatly to this decline. The defeat of the Paris Commune and the incipient reaction in France, which in a few years spread over Spain and Italy as well, pushed the fruitful idea of a council system for labour far into the background. The sections of the International in those countries were for a long time able to carry on only an underground existence and were obliged to concentrate all their strength on repelling the reaction. Only with the awakening of revolutionary Syndicalism in France were the creative ideas of the First International rescued from oblivion, once more to vitalise the Socialist labour movement.

Chapter 4. The Objectives of Anarchosyndicalism

Anarcho-Syndicalism versus political socialism; Political parties and labour unions; Federalism versus Centralism; Germany and Spain; The organisation of Anarcho-Syndicalism; The impotence of political parties for social reconstruction; The CNT in Spain: its aims and methods; Constructive work of the labour syndicates and peasant collectives in Spain; Anarcho-Syndicalism and national politics; Problems of our time.

Modern Anarcho-Syndicalism is a direct continuation of those social aspirations which took shape in the bosom of the First International and which were best understood and most strongly held by the libertarian wing of the great workers' alliance. Its present day representatives are the federations in the different countries of the revived *International Workingmen's Association* of 1922, the most important of which is the powerful Federation of Labour (*Confederación Nacional de Trabajo*) in Spain. Its theoretical assumptions are based on the teachings of Libertarian or Anarchist Socialism, while its form of organisation is largely borrowed from revolutionary Syndicalism, which in the years from 1900 to 1910 experienced a marked upswing, particularly in France. It stands in direct opposition to the political Socialism of our day, represented by the parliamentary labour parties in the different countries. While in the time of this First International barely the first beginnings of these parties existed in Germany, France and Switzerland, today we are in a position to estimate the results of their tactics for Socialism and the labour movement after more than sixty years' activity in all countries.

Participation in the politics of the bourgeois states has not brought the labour movement a hairs' breadth closer to Socialism, but, thanks to this method, Socialism has almost been completely crushed and condemned to insignificance. The ancient proverb: "Who eats of the pope, dies of him," has held true in this content also; who eats of the state is ruined by it. Participation in parliamentary politics has affected the Socialist labour movement like an insidious poison. It destroyed the belief in the necessity of constructive Socialist activity and, worst of all, the impulse to self-help, by inoculating people with the ruinous delusion that salvation always comes from above.

Thus, in place of the creative Socialism of the old International, there developed a sort of substitute product which has nothing in common with real Socialism but the name. Socialism steadily lost its character of a cultural ideal, which was to prepare the peoples for the dissolution of capitalist society, and, therefore, could not let itself be halted by the artificial frontiers of the national states. In the minds of the leaders of this new phase of the Socialist movement the interests of the national state were blended more and more with the alleged aims of their party, until at last they became unable to distinguish any definite boundaries between them. So inevitably the labour movement was gradually incorporated in the equipment of the national state and restored to this equilibrium which it had actually lost before.

It would be a mistake to find in this strange about-face an international betrayal by the leaders, as has so often been done. The truth is that we have to do here with a gradual assimilation to the modes of thought of capitalist society, which is a condition of the practical activities of the labour parties of today, and which necessarily affects the intellectual attitude of their political leaders. These very parties which had once set out to conquer Socialism saw themselves compelled by the iron logic of conditions to sacrifice their Socialist convictions bit by bit to the national policies of the state. They became, without the majority of their adherents ever becoming aware of it, political lightning rods for the security of the capitalist social order. The political power which they had wanted to conquer had gradually conquered their Socialism until there was scarcely anything left of it.

Parliamentarianism, which quickly attained a dominating position in the labour parties of the different countries, lured a lot of bourgeois minds and career-hungry politicians into the Socialist camp, and this helped to accelerate the internal decay of original Socialist principles. Thus Socialism in the course of time lost its creative initiative and became an ordinary reform movement which lacked any element of greatness. People were content with successes at the polls, and no longer attributed any importance to social upbuilding and constructive education of the workers for this end. The consequences of this disastrous neglect of one of the weightiest problems, one of decisive importance for the realisation of Socialism, were revealed in their full scope when after the World War, a revolutionary situation arose in many of the countries of Europe. The collapse of the old system had, in several states, put into the hands of the Socialists the power they had striven for so long and pointed to as the first prerequisite for the realisation of Socialism. In Russia the seizure of power by the left wing of state Socialism, in the form of Bolshevism paved the way, not for a Socialist society, but for the most primitive type of bureaucratic state capitalism and a reversion to the political absolutism which was long ago abolished in most countries by bourgeois revolutions. In Germany, however, where the moderate wing in the form of Social Democracy attained to power, Socialism, in its long years of absorption in routine parliamentary tasks, had become so bogged down that it was no longer capable of any creative act whatsoever. Even a bourgeois democratic sheet like the *Frankfurter Zeitung* felt obliged to confirm that "the history of European peoples has not previously produced a revolution that has been so poor in creative ideas and so weak in revolutionary energy."

But that was not all: not only was political Socialism in no position to undertake any kind of constructive effort in the direction of Socialism, it did not even possess the moral strength to hold on to the achievements of bourgeois Democracy and Liberalism, and surrendered the country without resistance to Fascism, which smashed the entire labour movement to bits with one blow. It had become so deeply immersed in the bourgeois state that it had lost all sense of constructive Socialist action and felt itself tied to the barren routine of everyday practical politics as a galley-slave was chained to his bench.

Modern Anarcho-Syndicalism is the direct reaction against the concepts and methods of political Socialism, a reaction which even before the war had already made itself manifest in the strong upsurge of the Syndicalist labour movement in France, Italy, and other countries, not to speak of Spain, where the great majority of the organised workers had always remained faithful to the doctrines of the First International.

The term "workers' syndicate" meant in France merely a trade union organisation of producers for the immediate betterment of their economic and social status. But the rise of revolutionary Syndicalism gave this original meaning a much wider and deeper import. Just as the part is, so to speak, the unified organisation for definite political effort within the modern constitutional state, and seeks to maintain the bourgeois order in one form or another, so, according to the Syndicalist view, the trade union, the syndicate, is the unified organisation of labour and has for its purpose the defence of the interests of the producers within existing society and the preparing for and the practical carrying out of the reconstruction of social life after the pattern of Socialism. It has, therefore, a double purpose: 1. As the fighting organisation of the workers against the employers to enforce the demands of the workers for the safeguarding and raising of their standard of living; 2. As the school for the intellectual training of the workers to make them acquainted with the technical management of production and economic life in general so that when a revolutionary situation arises they will be capable of taking the socio-economic organism into their own hands and remarking it according to Socialist principles.

Anarcho-Syndicalists are of the opinion that political parties, even when they bear a socialist name, are not fitted to perform either of these two tasks. The mere fact that, even in those countries where political Socialism commanded powerful organisations and had millions of voters behind it, the workers had never been able to dispense with trade unions because legislation offered them no protection in their struggle for daily bread, testifies to this. It frequently happened that in just these sections of the country where the Socialist parties were strongest the wages of workers were lowest and the conditions of labour worst. That was the case, for example, in the northern industrial districts of France, where Socialists were in the majority in numerous city administrations, and in Saxony and Silesia, where throughout its existence German Social Democracy had been able to show a large following.

Governments and parliaments seldom decide on economic or social reforms on their own initiative, and where this has happened thus far the alleged improvements have always remained a dead letter in the vast waste of laws. Thus the modest attempts of the English parliament in the early period of big industry, when the legislators, frightened by the horrible effects of the exploitation of children, at last resolved on some trifling amelioration's, for a long time had almost no effect. On the one hand they ran afoul of the lack of understanding of the workers themselves, on the other they were sabotaged outright by the employers. It was much the same with the well-known law which the Italian government enacted in the middle 90's to forbid women who were compelled to toil in the sulphur mines in Sicily from taking their children down into the mines with them. This law also remained a dead letter, because these unfortunate women were so poorly paid that they were obliged to disregard the law. Only a considerable time later, when these working women had succeeded in organising, and thus forcing up their standard of living, did the evil disappear of itself. There are plenty of similar instances in the history of every country.

But even the legal authorisation of a reform is no guarantee of its permanence unless there exist outside of parliament militant masses who are ready to defend it against every attack. Thus the English factory owners, despite the enactment of the ten-hour law in 1848, shortly afterward availed themselves of an industrial crisis to compel workers to toil for eleven or even twelve hours. When the factory inspectors took legal proceedings against individual employers on this account, the accused were not only acquitted, the Government hinted to the inspectors that they were not to insist on the letter of the law, so that the workers were obliged, after economic conditions had revived somewhat, to make the fight for the ten-hour day all over again on their own resources. Among the few economic improvements which the November Revolution of 1918 brought to the German workers, the eight-hour day was the most important. But it was snatched back from the workers by the employers in most industries, despite the fact that it was in the statutes, actually anchored legally in the Weimar Constitution itself.

But if political parties are absolutely incapable of making the slightest contribution to the improvement of the standard of living of the workers within present day society, they are far less capable to carry on the organic upbuilding of a Socialist community or even to pave the way for it, since they utterly lack every practical requirement for such an achievement. Russia and Germany have given quite sufficient proof of this.

The lancehead of the labour movement is, therefore, not the political party but the trader union, toughened by daily combat and permeated by Socialist spirit. Only in the realm of economy are the workers able to display their full social strength, for it is their activity as producers which holds together the whole social structure, and guarantees the existence of society at all. In any other field they are fighting on alien soil and wasting their strength in hopeless struggles which bring them not an iota nearer to the goal of their desires. in the field of parliamentary politics the worker is like the giant Antaeus of the Greek legend, whom Hercules was able to strangle after he took his feet off the earth who was his mother. Only as producer and creator of social wealth does he become aware of his strength; in solidaric union with his fellows he creates in the trade union the invincible phalanx which can withstand any assault, if it is aflame with the spirit of freedom and animated by the ideal of social justice.

For the Anarcho-Syndicalists the trade union is by no means a mere transitory phenomenon bound up with the duration of capitalist society, it is the germ of the Socialist society of the future, the elementary school of Socialism in general. Every new social structure makes organs for itself in the body of the old organism. Without this preliminary any social evolution is unthinkable. Even revolutions can only develop and mature the germs which already exist and have made their way into the consciousness of men; they cannot themselves create these germs or create new worlds out of nothing. It therefore concerns us to plant these germs while there is still yet time and bring them to the strongest possible development, so as to make the task of the coming social revolution easier and to ensure its permanence.

All the educational work of the Anarcho-Syndicalist is aimed at this purpose. Education for Socialism does not mean for them trivial campaign propaganda and so-called "politics-of-the-day," but the effort to make clear to the workers the intrinsic connections among social problems by technical instruction and the development of their administrative capacities, to prepare them for their rôle of re-shapers of economic life, and give them the moral assurance required for the performance of the task. No social body is better fitted for this purpose than the economic fighting organisations of the workers; it gives a definite direction to their social activities and toughens their resistance in the immediate struggle for the necessities of life and the defence of their human rights. This direct and unceasing warfare with the supporters of the present system develops at the same time the ethical concepts without which any social transformation is impossible: vital solidarity with their fellows-in-destiny and moral responsibility for their own actions.

Just because the educational work of the Anarcho-Syndicalists is directed toward the development of independent thought and action, they are outspoken opponents of all those centralising tendencies which are so characteristic of all political labour parties. But centralism, that artificial organisation from above which turns over the affairs of everybody in a lump to a small minority, is always attended by barren official routine; and this crushes individual conviction, kills all personal initiative by lifeless discipline and bureaucratic ossification, and permits no independent action. The organisation of Anarcho-Syndicalism is based on the principles of Federalism, on free combination from below upward, putting the right of self-determination of every member above everything else and recognising only the organic agreement of all on the basis of like interests and common convictions.

It has often been charged against federalism that it divides the forces and cripples the strength of organised resistance, and, very significantly, it has been just the representative of the political labour parties and of the trade unions under their influence who have kept repeating this charge to the point of nausea. But here, too, the facts of life have spoken more clearly than any theory. There was no country in the world where the whole labour movement was so completely centralised and the technique of organisation developed to such extreme perfection as in Germany before Hitler's accession to power. A powerful bureaucratic apparatus covered the whole country and determined every political and economic expression of the organised workers. In the very last elections the Social Democratic and Communist parties united over twelve million voters for their candidates. But after Hitler seized power six million organised workers did not raise a finger to avert the catastrophe which had plunged Germany into the abyss, and which in a few months beat their organisation completely to pieces.

But in Spain, where Anarcho-Syndicalism had maintained its hold upon organised labour from the days of the First International, and by untiring libertarian propaganda and sharp fighting had trained it to resistance, it was the powerful C.N.T. which by the boldness of its action frustrated the criminal plans of Franco and his numerous helpers at home and abroad, and by their heroic example spurred the Spanish workers and peasants to the battle against Fascism — a fact which Franco himself has been compelled to acknowledge. Without the heroic resistance of the Anarcho-Syndicalist labour unions the Fascist reactions would in a few weeks have dominated the whole country.

When one compares the technique of the federalist organisation of the C.N.T. with the centralistic machine which the German workers had built for themselves, one is surprised by the simplicity of the former. In the smaller syndicates every task for the organisation was performed voluntarily. In the larger alliances, where naturally established official representatives were necessary, these were elected for one year only and received the same pay as the workers in their trade. Even the General Secretary of the C.N.T. was no exception to this rule. this is an old tradition which has been kept up in Spain since the days of the International. This simple form of organisation not only sufficed the Spanish workers for turning the C.N.T. into a fighting unit of the first rank, it also safeguarded them against any bureaucratic regime in their own ranks and helped them to display that irresistible spirit of solidarity and tenaciousness which is so characteristic of this organisation, and which one encounters in no other country.

For the state centralisation is the appropriate form of organisation, since it aims at the greatest possible uniformity in social life for the maintenance of political and social equilibrium. But for a movement whose very existence depends on prompt action at any favourable moment and on the independent thought and action of its supporters, centralism could but be a curse by weakening its power of decision and systematically repressing all immediate action. If, for example, as was the case in Germany, every local strike had first to be approved by the Central, which was often hundreds of mils away and was not usually not in a position to pass a correct judgement on the local conditions, one cannot wonder that the inertia of the apparatus of organisation renders a quick attack quite impossible, and there thus arises a state of affairs where the energetic and intellectually alert groups no longer serve as patterns for the less active, but are condemned by these to inactivity, inevitably bringing the whole movement to stagnation. Organisation is, after all, only a means to an end. When it becomes an end in itself, it kills the spirit and the vital initiative of its members and sets up that domination by mediocrity which is the characteristic of all bureaucracies.

Anarcho-Syndicalists are, therefore, of the opinion that trade union organisation should be of such a character as to afford workers the possibility of achieving the utmost in their struggle against the employers, and at the same time provide them with a basis from which they will be able in a revolutionary position to proceed with reshaping of economic and social life.

Their organisation is accordingly constructed on the following principles: The workers in each locality join the unions for their respective trades, and these are subject to the veto of no Central but enjoy the entire right of self-determination. The trade unions of a city or rural district combine in a so-called labour cartel. The labour cartels constitute the centres for local propaganda and education; they weld the workers together as a class and prevent the rise of any narrow-minded factional spirit. In times of local labour trouble they arrange for the solidaric co-operation of the whole body of organised labour in the use of every agency available under the circumstances. All the labour cartels are grouped according to districts and regions to form the National Federation of Labour Cartels, which maintain the permanent connection between the local bodies, arranges for free adjustment of the productive labour of the members of the different organisations on co-operative lines, provide for the necessary co-operation in the field of education, in which the stronger cartels will need to come to the aid of the weaker ones, and in general support the local groups with council and guidance.

Every trade union is, moreover, federatively allied with all the same organisations in the same trade throughout the country, and these in turn with all related trades, so that all are combined in general industrial alliances. It is the task of these alliances to arrange for the co-operative action of the local groups, to conduct solidaric strikes where the necessity arises, and to meet all the demands of the day-to-day struggle between capital and labour. Thus the Federation of Labour Cartels and the Federation of Industrial Alliances constitute the two poles about which the whole life of the trade unions revolves.

Such a form of organisation not only gives the workers every opportunity for direct action in their struggles for daily bread, it also provides them with the necessary preliminaries for carrying through the reorganisation of social life on a Socialist plan by their own strength and without alien intervention, in case of a revolutionary crisis. Anarcho-Syndicalists are convinced that a Socialist economic order cannot be created by the decrees and statutes of a government, but only by the solidaric collaboration of the workers with hand or brain in each special branch of production; that is, through the taking over of the management of all plants by the producers themselves under such form that the separate groups, plants and branches of industry are independent members of the general economic organism and systematically carry on production and the distribution of the products in the interest of the community on the basis of free mutual agreements.

In such a case the labour cartels would take over the existing social capital in each community, determine the needs of the inhabitants of their districts, and organise local consumption. Through the agency of the national Federation of Labour Cartels it would be possible to calculate the total requirements of the country and adjust the work of production accordingly. On the other hand, it would be the task of the Industrial Alliances to take control of all the instruments of production, machines, raw materials, means of transportation and the like, and to provide the separate producing groups with what they need. In a word:

1. Organisation of the plants by the producers themselves and direction of the work by labour councils elected by them.
2. Organisation of the total production of the country by the industrial and agricultural alliances.
3. Organisation of consumption by the Labour Cartels.

In this respect, also practical experience has given the best instruction. It has shown us that economic questions in the Socialist meaning cannot be solved by a government, even when that is meant the celebrated *dictatorship of the proletariat*. In Russia the Bolshevist dictatorship stood for almost two whole years helpless before its economic problems and tried to hide its incapacity behind a flood of decrees and ordinances, of which ninety-nine percent were buried at once in the various bureaus. If the world could be set free by decrees, there would long ago have been no problems left in Russia. In its fanatical zeal for government, Bolshevism has violently destroyed just the most valuable beginnings of a Socialist social order, by suppressing the co-operatives, bringing the trade unions under state control, and depriving the soviets of their independence almost from the beginning. Kropotkin said with justice in his "Message to the Workers of the West European Countries":

> "Russia has shown us the way in which Socialism cannot be realised, although the populace, nauseated with the old regime, opposed no active resistance to the experiments of the new government. The idea of the workers' councils for the control of the political and economic life is, in itself, of extraordinary importance...But so long as the country is dominated by the dictatorship of a party, the workers' and peasants' councils naturally lose their significance. They are thereby degraded to the same passive rôle which the representatives of the estates used to play in the time of the absolute monarchies. A workers' council ceases to be a free and valuable adviser when no free press exists in the country, as has been the case with us for over two years. Worse still: the workers' and peasants' councils lose all their meaning when no public propaganda takes place before their election, and the elections themselves are conducted under the pressure of party dictatorship. Such a government by councils (soviet government) amounts to a definite step backward as soon as the Revolution advances to the erection of new society on a new economic basis: it becomes just a dead principle on a dead foundation."

The course of events has proved Kropotkin right on every point. Russia is today farther from Socialism than any other country. Dictatorship does not lead to the economic and social liberation of the toiling masses, but to the suppression of even the most trivial freedom and the development of an unlimited despotism which respects no rights and treads underfoot every feeling of human dignity. What the Russian worker has gained economically under this regime is a most ruinous form of human exploitation, borrowed from the most extreme stage of capitalism, in the shape of the Stakhanov system, which raises his productive capacity to its highest limit and degrades him to galley slave, who is denied all control of his personal labour, and who must submit to every order of his superiors if he does not wish to expose himself to penalties life and liberty. But compulsory labour is the last road that can lead to Socialism. It estranges the man from the community, destroys his joy in his daily work, and stifles that sense of personal responsibility to his fellows without which there can be no talk of Socialism at all.

We shall not even speak of Germany here. One could not reasonably expect of a party like the Social Democrats — whose central organ *Vorwärts*, just on the evening before the November Revolution of 1918 warned the workers against precipitancy, "as the German people are not ready for a republic" — that it would experiment with Socialism. Power, we might say, fell into its lap overnight, and it actually did not know what to do with it. Its absolute impotence contributed not a little to enabling Germany to bask today in the sun of the *Third Reich*.

The Anarcho-Syndicalist labour unions of Spain, and especially of Catalonia, where their influence is strongest, have shown us an example in this respect which is unique in the history of Socialist labour movement. In this they have only confirmed what the Anarcho-Syndicalists have always insisted on: that the approach to Socialism is possible only when the workers have created the necessary organism for it, and when above all they have previously prepared for it by a genuinely Socialistic education and direct action. But this was the case in Spain, where since the days of the International the weight of the labour movement had lain, not in political parties, but in the revolutionary trade unions.

When, on July 19, 1936, the conspiracy of the Fascist generals ripened into open revolt and was put down in a few days by the heroic resistance of the C.N.T.(National Federation of Labour) and the F.A.I.(Anarchist Federation of Iberia), ridding Catalonia of the enemy and frustrating the plan of the conspirators, based as it was on sudden surprise, it was clear that the Catalonian workers would not stop halfway. So there followed the collectivising of the land and the taking over of the plants by the workers' and peasants' syndicates; and this movement, which was released by the initiative of the C.N.T. and the F.A.I., with irresistible power overran Aragon, the Levante and other sections of the country, and even swept along with it a large part of the trade unions of the Socialist Party, organised in the U.G.T. (General Labour Union). The revolt of the Fascists had set Spain on the road to a social revolution.

This same event reveals that the Anarcho-Syndicalist workers of Spain not only know how to fight, but that they are filled with that great constructive spirit derived from their many years of Socialist education. It is the great merit of Libertarian Socialism in Spain, which now finds expression in the C.N.T. and F.A.I., that since the days of the First International it has trained the workers in that spirit which treasures freedom above all else and regards the intellectual independence of its adherents as the basis of its existence. The libertarian labour movement in Spain has never lost itself in the labyrinth of an economic metaphysics which crippled its intellectual buoyancy by fatalistic conceptions, as was the case in Germany; nor has it unprofitably wasted its energy in the barren routine tasks of bourgeois parliaments. Socialism was for it a concern of the people, an organic growth proceeding from the activity of the masses themselves and having its basis in their economic organisations.

Therefore the C.N.T. is not simply an alliance of industrial workers like the trade unions in every other country. It embraces within its ranks also the syndicates of the peasant and fieldworkers as well as those of the brain workers and the intellectuals. If the Spanish peasants are now fighting shoulder to shoulder with city workers against Fascism, it is the result of the great work of Socialist education which has been performed by the C.N.T. and its forerunners. Socialists of all schools, genuine liberals and bourgeois anti-fascists who have had an opportunity to observe on the spot have thus far passed only one judgement on the creative capacity of the C.N.T. and have accorded to its constructive labours the highest admiration. Not one of them could help extolling the natural intelligence, the thoughtfulness and prudence, and above all the unexampled tolerance with which the workers and peasants of the C.N.T. have gone about their difficult task.[1] Workers, peasants, technicians and men of science had come together for co-operative work, and in three months gave an entirely new character to the whole economic life of Catalonia.

In Catalonia today three-fourths of the land is collectivised and co-operatively cultivated by the workers' syndicates. In this each community presents a type by itself and adjusts its internal affairs in its own way, but settles its economic questions through the agency of its Federation. Thus there is preserved the possibility of free enterprise, inciting new ideas and mutual stimulation. One-fourth of the country is in the hands of small peasant proprietors, to whom has been left the free choice between joining the collectives or continuing their family husbandry. In many instances their small holdings have even been increased in proportion to the size of their families. In Aragon an overwhelming majority of the peasants declared for collective cultivation. There are in that province over four hundred collective farms, of which about ten are under the control of the Socialist U.G.T., while all the rest are conducted by syndicates of the C.N.T. Agriculture has made such advances there that in the course of a year forty per cent of the formerly untilled

---

[1] Here are just a few opinions of foreign journalists who have no personal connection with the Anarchist movement. Thus, Andrea Oltmares, professor in the University of Geneva, in the course of an address of some length, said: *"In the midst of the civil war the Anarchists have proved themselves to be political organisers of the first rank. They kindled in everyone the required sense of responsibility, and knew how, by eloquent appeals, to keep alive the spirit of sacrifice for the general welfare of the people." "As a Social Democrat I speak here with inner joy and sincere admiration of my experiences in Catalonia. The anti-capitalist transformation took place here without their having to resort to a dictatorship. The members of the syndicates are their own masters and carry on the production and the distribution of the products of labour under their own management, with the advice of technical experts in whom they have confidence. The enthusiasm of the workers is so great that they scorn any personal advantage and are concerned only for the welfare of all."* The well-known anti-Fascist, Carlo Roselli, who before Mussolini's accession to power was Professor of Economics in the University of Genoa, put his judgement into the following words: *"In three months Catalonia has been able to set up a new social order on the ruins of an ancient system. This is chiefly due to the Anarchists, who have revealed a quite remarkable sense of proportion, realistic understanding, and organising ability...all the revolutionary forces of Catalonia have united in a program of Syndicalist-Socialist character: socialisation of large industry; recognition of the small proprietor, workers' control...Anarcho-Syndicalism, hitherto so despised, has revealed itself as a great constructive force...I am not an Anarchist, but I regard it as my duty to express here my opinion of the Anarchists of Catalonia, who have all too often been represented to the world as a destructive, if not criminal, element. I was with them at the front, in the trenches, and I have learnt to admire them. The Catalonian Anarchists belong to the advance guard of the coming revolution. A new world was born with them, and it is a joy to serve that world."* And Fenner Brockway, Secretary of the I.L.P. in England who travelled to Spain after the May events in Catalonia (1937), expressed his impressions in the following words: *"I was impressed by the strength of the C.N.T. It was unnecessary to tell me that it was the largest and most vital of the working-class organisations in Spain. The large industries were clearly, in the main, in the hands of the C.N.T. — railways, road transport, shipping, engineering, textiles, electricity, building, agriculture. At Valencia the U.G.T. had a larger share of control than at Barcelona, but generally speaking the mass of manual workers belonged to the C.N.T. The U.G.T. membership was more of the type of the 'white-collar' worker...I was immensely impressed by the constructive revolutionary work which is being done by the C.N.T. Their achievement of workers' control in industry is an inspiration. One could take the example of the railways or engineering or textiles...There are still some Britishers and Americans who regard the Anarchists of Spain as impossible, undisciplined, uncontrollable. This is poles away from the truth. The Anarchists of Spain, through the C.N.T., are doing one of the biggest constructive jobs ever done by the working class. At the front they are fighting Fascism. Behind the front they are actually constructing the new Workers' Society. They see that the war against Fascism and the carrying through of the Social Revolution are inseparable. Those who have seen and understand what they are doing must honour them and be grateful to them. They are resisting Fascism. They are at the same time creating the New Workers' Order which is the only alternative to Fascism. That is surely the biggest things now being done by the workers in any part of the world."* And in another place: *"The great solidarity that existed amongst the Anarchists was due to each individual relying on his own strength and not depending on leadership. The organisations must, to be successful, be combined with a free-thinking people; not a mass, but free individuals."*

land has been brought under cultivation. In the Levante, in Andalusia and Castile, also, collective agriculture under the management of the syndicates is making constantly greater advances. In numerous smaller communities a Socialist form of life has already become naturalised, the inhabitants no longer carrying on exchange by means of money, but satisfying their needs out of the product of their collective industry and conscientiously devoting the surplus to their comrades fighting at the front.

In most of the rural collectives individual compensation for work performed has been retained, and the further upbuilding of the new system postponed until the termination of the war, which at present claims the entire strength of the people. In these the amount of the wages is determined by the size of the families. The economic reports in the daily bulletins of the C.N.T. are extremely interesting, with their accounts of the building up of the collectives and their technical development through the introduction of machines and chemical fertilisers, which had been almost unknown before. The agricultural collectives in Castile alone have during the past year spent more than two million pasetas for this purpose. The great task of collectivising the land was made much easier after the rural federations of the U.G.T. joined the general movement. In many communities all affairs are arranged by delegates of the C.N.T. and the U.G.T., bringing about a rapprochement of the two organisations which culminated in an alliance of the workers in the two organisations.

But the workers' syndicates have made their most astounding achievements in the field in industry, since they took into their hands the administration of industrial life as a whole. In Catalonia in the course of a year the railroads were fitted out with a complete modern equipment, and in punctuality the service reached a point that had been hitherto unknown. The same advances were achieved in the entire transport system, in the textile industry, in machine construction, in building, and in the small industries. But in the war industries the syndicates have performed a genuine miracle. By the so-called neutrality pact the Spanish Government was prevented from importing from abroad any considerable amount of war materials. But Catalonia before the Fascist revolt not a single plant for the manufacture of army equipment. The first concern, therefore, was to remake whole industries to meet the war demands. A hard task for the syndicates, which already had in their hands full setting up of a new social order. But they perfumed it with an energy and a technical efficiency that can be explained only by the workers and their boundless readiness to make sacrifices for their cause. Men toiled in the factories twelve and fourteen hours a day to bring the great work to completion. Today Catalonia possesses 283 huge plants which are operating day and night in the production of war materials, so that the fronts may be kept supplied. At present Catalonia is providing for the greater part of all war demands. Professor Andres Oltmares declared in the course of an article that in this field the workers' syndicates of Catalonia "had accomplished in seven weeks as much as France did in fourteen months after the outbreak of the World War."

But that is not all by a great deal. The unhappy war brought into Catalonia an overwhelming flood of fugitives from all the war-swept districts in Spain; their number has today grown to a million. Over fifty per cent of the sick and wounded in the hospitals of Catalonia are not Catalonians. One understands, therefore, with what a task the workers' syndicates were confronted in the meeting of all these demands. Of the re-organisation of the whole educational system by the teachers' groups in the C.N.T., the associations for the protection of works of art, and a hundred other matters we cannot even make mention here.

During this same time the C.N.T. was maintaining 120,000 of its militia, who were fighting on all fronts. No other organisation has thus far made such sacrifices of life and limb as the C.N.T.-F.A.I. In its heroic stand against Fascism it has lost a lot of its most distinguished fighters, among them Francisco Asco and Buenaventura Durutti, whose epic greatness made him the hero of the Spanish people.

Under these circumstances it is, perhaps, understandable that the syndicates have not thus far been able to bring to completion their great task of social reconstruction, and for the time being were unable to give their full attention to the organisation of consumption. The war, the possession by the Fascist armies of important sources of raw materials, the German and Italian invasion, the hostile attitude of foreign capital, the onslaughts of the counter-revolution in the country itself, which, significantly, was befriended this time by Russia and the Communist Party of Spain — all this and many other things have compelled the syndicates to postpone many great and important tasks until the war is brought to a victorious conclusion. But by taking the land and the industrial plants under their own management they have taken the first and most important step on the road to Socialism. Above all, they have proved *that the workers, even without the capitalist, are able to carry on production and to do it better than a lot of profit-hungry entrepreneurs.* Whatever the outcome of the bloody war in Spain may be, to have given this great demonstration remains the indisputable service of the Spanish Anarcho-Syndicalists, whose heroic example has opened for the Socialist movement new outlooks for the future.

If the Anarcho-Syndicalists are striving to implant in the working classes in every country an understanding of this new form of constructive Socialism, and to show them that they must, today, give to their economic fighting organisations the forms to enable them during a general economic crisis to carry through the work of Socialist upbuilding, this does not mean that these forms must everywhere be cut to the same pattern. In every country there are special conditions which are intimately intergrown with its historical development, its traditions, and its peculiar psychological assumptions. The great superiority of Federalism is, indeed, just that it takes these important matters into account and does not insist on a uniformity that does violence to free thought, and forces on men from without things contrary to their inner inclinations.

Kropotkin once said that, taking England as an example, there existed three great movements which, at the time of a revolutionary crisis would enable the workers to carry through a complete overturn of social economy: trades unionism, the co-operative organisations, and the movement for municipal Socialism; provided that they had a fixed goal in view and worked together according to a definite plan. The workers must learn that, not only must their social liberation be their own work, but that liberation was possible only if they themselves attended to the constructive preliminaries instead of leaving the task to the politicians, who were in no way fitted for it. And above all they must understand that however different the immediate preliminaries for their liberation might be in different countries, the effect of capitalist exploitation are everywhere the same and they must, therefore, give to their efforts the necessary international character.

Above all they must not tie up these efforts with the interests of the national states, as has, unfortunately, happened in most countries hitherto. The world of organised labour must pursue its own ends, as it has its own interests to defend, and these are not identical with the state or those of the possessing classes. A collaboration of workers and employees such as was advocated by the Socialist Party and the trade unions in Germany after the World War can only result in the workers being condemned to the role of the poor Lazarus, who must be content to eat the crumbs that fall from the rich man's table. Collaboration is possible only where the ends and, most importantly of all, the interests are the same.

No doubt some small comforts may sometimes fall to the share of the workers when the bourgeoisie of their country attain some advantage over that of another country; but this always happens at the cost of their own freedom and the economic oppression of other peoples. The worker in England, France, Holland, and so on, participates to some extent in the profits which, without efforts on their part, fall into the laps of the bourgeoisie of his country from the unrestrained exploitation of colonial peoples; but sooner or later there comes the time when these people, too, wake up, and he has to pay all the more dearly for the small advantages he has enjoyed. Events in Asia will show this still more clearly in the near future. Small gains arising for increased opportunity of employment and higher wages may accrue to the worker in a successful state from the carving out of new markets at the cost of others; but at the same time their brothers on the other side of the border have to pay for them by unemployment and the lowering of their standard of living. The result is an ever widening rift in the international labour movement, which not even the loveliest resolutions by international congresses can put out of existence. By this rift the liberation of the workers from the yoke of wage-slavery is pushed further and further into the distance. As long as the worker ties up his interests with those of the bourgeoisie of his country instead of with those of his class, he must logically also take in his stride all the results of that relationship. He must stand ready to fight the wars of the possessing classes for the retention and extension of their markets, and to defend any injustice they may perpetrate on other peoples. The Socialist press of Germany was merely being consistent when, at the time of the World War, they urged the annexation of foreign territory. This was merely the inevitable result of the intellectual attitude and the methods which the political labour parties had pursued for a long time before the war. Only when the workers in every country shall come to understand clearly that their interests are everywhere the same, and out of this understanding learn to act together, will the effective basis be laid for the international liberation of the working class.

Every time has its particular problems and its own peculiar methods of solving these problems. The problem that is set for our time is that of freeing man from the curse of economic exploitation and political and social enslavement. The era of political revolution is over, and where such still occur they do not alter in the least the bases of the capitalist social order. On the one hand it becomes constantly clearer that bourgeois democracy is so degenerate that it is no longer capable of offering effective resistance to the threat of Fascism. On the other hand political Socialism has lost itself so completely on the dry channels of bourgeois politics that it no longer has any sympathy with the genuinely Socialistic education of the masses and never rises above the advocacy of petty reforms. But the development of capitalism and the modern big state have brought us today to a situation where we are driving on under full sail toward a universal catastrophe. The last World War and its economic and social consequences, which are today working more and more disastrously, and which have grown into a definite danger to the very existence of all human culture, are sinister signs of the times which no man of insight can misinterpret. It therefore concerns us today to reconstruct the economic life of the peoples from the ground up and build it up anew in the spirit of Socialism. But only the producers themselves are fitted for this task, since they are the only value-creating element in society out of which a new future can arise. Theirs must be the task of freeing labour from all the fetters which economic exploitation has fastened on it, of freeing society from all the institutions and procedures of political power, and of opening the way to an alliance of free groups of men and women based on co-operative labour and a planned administration of things in the interests of the community. To prepare the toiling masses in city and country for this great goal and to bind them together as a militant force is the objective of modern Anarcho-Syndicalism, and in this its whole purpose is exhausted.

Chapter 5. The Methods of Anarcho-Syndicalism

Anarcho-Syndicalism and political action; The Significance of political rights; Direct Action versus Parliamentarism; The strike and its meaning for the workers; The Sympathetic Strike; The General Strike; The Boycott; Sabotage by the workers; Sabotage by capitalism; The social strike as a means of social protection; Anti-militarism.

It has often been charged against Anarcho-Syndicalism that it has no interest in the political structure of the different countries, and consequently no interest in the political struggles of the time, and confines its activities to the fight for purely economic demands. This idea is altogether erroneous and springs either from outright ignorance or wilful distortion of the facts. It is not the political struggle as such which distinguishes the Anarcho-Syndicalists from the modern labour parties, both in principle and in tactics, but the form of this struggle and the aims which it has in view. They by no means rest content with the ideal of a future society without lordship; their efforts are also directed, even today, at restricting the activities of the state and blocking its influence in every department of social life wherever they see an opportunity. It is these tactics which mark off Anarcho-Syndicalist procedure from the aims and methods of the political labour parties, all of whose activities tend constantly to broaden the sphere of influence of the political power of the state and to extend it in ever increasing measure over the economic life of society. But by this, in the outcome, the way is merely prepared for an era of state capitalism, which according to all experience may be just the opposite of what Socialism is actually fighting for.

The attitude of Anarcho-Syndicalism toward the political power of the present-day state is exactly the same as it takes toward the system of capitalist exploitation. Its adherents are perfectly clear that the social injustices of that system rest, not on its unavoidable excrescences, but in the capitalistic economic order as such. But, while their efforts are directed at abolishing the existing form of capitalist exploitation and replacing it by a Socialist order, they never for a moment forget to work also by every means at their command to lower the rate of profit of the capitalists under existing conditions, and to raise the producer's share of the products of his labour to the highest possible.

Anarcho-Syndicalists pursue the same tactics in their fight against that political power which finds its expression in the state. They recognise that the modern state is just the consequence of capitalist economic monopoly, and the class divisions which this has set up in society, and merely serves the purpose of maintaining this status by every oppressive instrument of political power. But, while they are convinced that along with the system of exploitation its political protective device, the state, will also disappear, to give place to the administration of public affairs on the basis of free agreement, they do not all overlook that the efforts of the worker within the existing political order must always be directed toward defending all achieved political and social rights against every attack of reaction, constantly widening the scope of these rights wherever the opportunity for this presents itself.

For just as the worker cannot be indifferent to the economic conditions of his life in existing society, so he cannot remain indifferent to the political structure of his country. Both in the struggle for his daily bread and for every kind of propaganda looking toward his social liberation he needs political rights and liberties, and he must fight for these himself in every situation where they are denied him, and must defend them with all his strength whenever the attempt is made to wrest them from him. It is, therefore, utterly absurd to assert that the Anarcho-Syndicalists take no interest in the political struggles of the time. The heroic battle of the C.N.T. in Spain against Fascism is, perhaps, the best proof that there is not a grain of truth in this idle talk.

But the point of attack in the political struggle lies, not in the legislative bodies, but in the people. Political rights do not originate in parliaments; they are, rather, forced on parliaments from without. And even their enactment into law has for a long time been no guarantee of their security. Just as the employers always try to nullify every concession they had made to labour as soon as opportunity offered, as soon as any signs of weakness were observable in the workers' organisations, so governments also are always inclined to restrict or to abrogate completely rights and freedoms that have been achieved if they imagine that the people will put up no resistance. Even in these countries where such things as freedom of the press, right of assembly, right of combination and the like have long existed, governments are constantly trying to restrict these rights or to reinterpret them by juridical hair-splitting. Political rights do not exist because they have been legally set down on a piece of paper, but only when they have become the ingrown habit of a people, and when any attempt to impair them will meet with the violent resistance of the populace. Where this is not the case, there is no help in any parliamentary Opposition or any Platonic appeals to the constitution. One compels respect from others when he knows how to defend his dignity as a human being. This is not only true in private life, it has always been the same in political life as well.

The peoples owe all the political rights and privileges which we enjoy today in greater or lesser measure, not to the good will of their governments, but to their own strength. Governments have employed every means that lay in their power to prevent the attainment of these rights or to render them illusory. Great mass movements among the people and whole revolutions have been necessary to wrest these rights from the ruling classes, who would never have consented to them voluntarily. One need only study the history of the past three hundred years to understand by what relentless struggles every right has to be wrested inch by inch from the despots. What hard struggles, for example, had the workers in England, France, Spain, and other countries to endure to compel their governments to recognise the right of trade union organisation. In France the prohibition against trade unions persisted until 1886. Had it not been for the incessant struggles of the workers, there would be no right of combination in the French Republic even today. Only after the workers had by direct action confronted parliament with accomplished facts, did the government see itself obliged to take the new situation into account and give legal sanction to the trade unions. *What is important is not that governments have decided to concede certain rights to the people, but the reason why they have had to do this.* To him who fails to understand the connection here history will always remain a book with seven seals.

Of course, if one accepts Lenin's phrase and thinks of freedom as merely a "bourgeois prejudice," then, to be sure, political rights and liberties have no value at all for the workers. But then all the countless struggles of the past, all the revolts and revolutions to which we owe these rights, are also without value. To proclaim this bit of wisdom it would hardly have been necessary to overthrow tsarism, for even the censorship of Nicholas II would certainly have had no objection to the designation of freedom as a "bourgeois prejudice." Moreover, the great theorists of reaction, Joseph de Maistre and Louis Bonald, has already done this, though in different words, and the defenders of absolutism had been very grateful to them.

But the Anarcho-Syndicalists would be the every last to mistake the importance of these rights to the workers. If they, nevertheless, reject any participation in the work of bourgeois parliaments, it is not because they have no sympathy with political struggles in general, but because they are firmly convinced that parliamentary activity is for the workers the very weakest and the most hopeless form of the political struggle. For the bourgeois classes the parliamentary system is without a doubt an appropriate instrument for the settlement of such conflicts as arise, and for making profitable collaboration possible, as they are all equally interested in maintaining the existing economic order and the political organisation for the protection of that order. Now, where a common interest exists, a mutual agreement is possible and serviceable to all parties. But for the working class the situation is very different. For them the existing economic order is the source of their economic exploitation, and the organised power of the state the instrument of their political and social subjection. Even the freest ballot cannot do away with the glaring contrast between the possessing and non-possessing classes in society. It can only serve to impart to a system of social injustice the stamp of legal right and to induce the slave to set the stamp of legality on his own servitude.

But, most important of all, practical experience has shown that the participation of the workers in parliamentary activity cripples their power of resistance and dooms to futility their warfare against the existing system. Parliamentary participation has not brought the workers one iota nearer to their final goal; it has even prevented them from protecting the rights they have won against the attacks of the reaction. In Prussia, for example, the largest state in Germany, where the Social Democrats until shortly before Hitler's accession to power were the strongest party in the government and had control of the most important ministries in the country, Herr von Papen, after his appointment as Reichskanzler by Hindenburg, could venture to violate the constitution of the land and dissolve the Prussian ministry with only a lieutenant and a dozen soldiers. When the Socialist Party in its helplessness could think of nothing to do after this open breach of the constitution except to appeal to the high court of the Reich instead of meeting the perpetrators of the *coup d'etat* with open resistance, the reaction knew they had nothing more to fear and from then on could offer the workers what they pleased. The fact is that von Papen's *coup d'etat* was merely the start along the road to the Third Reich.

Anarcho-Syndicalists, then, are not in any way opposed to the political struggle, but in their opinion this struggle, too, must take the form of direct action, in which the instruments of economic power which the working class has at its command are the most effective. The most trivial wage fight shows clearly that, whenever the employers find themselves in difficulties, the state steps in with the police, and even in some cases with the militia, to protect the threatened interests of the possessing classes. It would, therefore, be absurd for them to overlook the importance of the political struggle. Every event that affects the life of the community is of a political nature. In this sense, every important economic action, such, for example, as a general strike, is also a political action and, moreover, one of incomparably greater importance than any parliamentary proceeding. Of a political nature is likewise the battle of the Anarcho-Syndicalists against Fascism and the anti-militarist propaganda, a battle which for decades was carried on solely by the libertarian Socialists and the Syndicalists, and which was attended by tremendous sacrifices.

The fact is that, when the Socialist labour parties have wanted to achieve some decisive political reform, they have always found that they could not do so by their own strength and have been obliged to rely wholly on the economic fighting power of the working class. The political general strikes in Belgium, Sweden and Austria for the attainment of universal suffrage are proof of this. And in Russia it was the great general strike of the working people that in 1905 pressed the pen into the tsar's hand for the signing of the constitution. What the heroic struggle of the Russian intelligentsia had not been able to accomplish in decades, the united economic action of the working classes quickly brought to fulfilment.

The focal point of the political struggle lies, then, not in the political parties, but in the economic fighting organisations of the workers. It as the recognition of this which impelled the Anarcho-Syndicalists to centre all their activity on the Socialist education of the masses and on the utilisation of their economic and social power. Their method is that of direct action in both the economic and the political struggles of the time. That is the only method which has been able to achieve anything at all in every decisive moment in history. And the bourgeoisie in its struggles against absolutism has also made abundant use of this method, and by refusal to pay taxes, by boycott and revolution, has defiantly asserted its position as the dominant class in society. So much the worse if its representatives of today have forgotten the story of their fathers, and howl bloody murder at the "unlawful methods" of the workers fighting for liberation. As if the law had ever permitted a subject class to shake off its yoke.

By direct action the Anarcho-Syndicalists mean every method of immediate warfare by the workers against their economic and political oppressors. Among these the outstanding are: the strike, in all its gradations from the simple wage-struggle to the general strike; the boycott; sabotage in its countless forms; anti-militarist propaganda; and in particularly critical cases, such, for example, as that in Spain today, armed resistance of the people for the protection of life and liberty.

Among these fighting techniques the strike, that is, organised refusal to work, is the most used. It plays in the industrial age the same rôle for the workers as did their frequent uprisings for the peasants in the feudal era. In its simplest form it is for the workers an indispensable means of raising their standard of living or defending their attained advantages against the concerted measures of the employers. But the strike is for the workers not only a means for the defence of immediate economic interests, it is also a continuous schooling for their powers of resistance, showing them every day that every least right has to be won by unceasing struggle against the existing system.

Just as are the economic fighting organisations of the workers, so also are the daily wage-struggles a result of the capitalist economic order, and consequently, a vital necessity for the workers. Without these they would be submerged in the abyss of poverty. Certainly the social problem cannot be solved by wage-struggles alone, but they are the best educative equipment for making the workers aquainted with the real essence of the social problem, training them for the struggle for liberation from economic and social slavery. It may also be taken as true that so long as the worker has to sell hands and brain to an employer, he will in the long run never earn more than is required to provide the most indispensable necessities of life. But these necessities of life are not always the same, but are constantly changing with the demands which the worker makes on life.

Here we come to the general cultural significance of the labour struggle. The economic alliance of the producers not only afford them a weapon for the enforcement of better living conditions, it becomes for them a practical school, a university of experience, from which they draw instruction and enlightenment in richest measure. The practical experiences and occurrences of the everyday struggles of the workers find an intellectual precipitate in their organisations, deepen their understanding, and broaden their intellectual outlook. By the constant intellectual elaboration of their life experiences there are developed in individuals new needs and the urge for different fields of intellectual life. And precisely in this development lies the great cultural significance of these struggles.

True intellectual culture and the demand for higher interests in life does not become possible until man has achieved a certain material standard of living, which makes him capable of these. Without this preliminary any higher intellectual aspirations are quite out of the question. Men who are constantly threatened by direst misery can hardly have much understanding of the higher cultural values. Only after the workers, by decades of struggle, had conquered for themselves a better standard of living could there be any talk of intellectual and cultural development among them. But it is just these aspirations of the workers which the employers view with deepest distrust. For capitalists as a class, the well-known saying of the Spanish minister, Juan Bravo Murillo, still holds good today: "*We need no men who can think among the workers; what we need is beasts of toil.*"

One of the most important results of the daily economic struggles is the development of solidarity among the workers, and this has for them a quite different meaning from the political coalition of parties whose following is composed of people of every social class. A feeling of mutual helpfulness, whose strength is constantly being renewed in the daily struggle for the necessities of life, which is constantly making the most extreme demands on the co-operation of men subjected to the same conditions, operates very differently from abstract party principles, which for the most part are of only Platonic value. It grows into the vital consciousness of a community of fate, and this gradually develops into a new sense of right, and becomes the preliminary ethical assumption of every effort at the liberation of an oppressed class.

To cherish and strengthen this natural solidarity of the workers and to give to every strike movement a more profoundly social character, is one of the most important tasks which the Anarcho-Syndicalists have set themselves. For this reason the sympathetic strike is one of their choicest weapons, and has developed in Spain to a compass it has not attained in any other country. Through it the economic battle becomes a deliberate action of the workers as a class. The sympathetic strike is the collaboration of related, but also of unrelated, categories of labour, to help the battle of a particular trade to victory by extending the strike to other branches of labour, where this is necessary. In this case the workers are not satisfied with giving fighting assistance to their striking brethren, but go further, and by crippling entire industries cause a break in the whole economic life in order to make their demands effective.

Today, when by the formation of national and international cartels and trusts private capitalism grows more and more into monopoly capitalism, this form of warfare is in most cases the only one by which the workers can still promise themselves success. Because of the internal transformation in industrial capitalism the sympathetic strike becomes for the workers the imperative of the hour. Just as the employers in their cartels and protective organisations are building an ever broader basis for the defence of their interests, so also the workers must turn their attention to creating for themselves by an ever wider alliance of their national and international economic organisations the required basis for solidaric mass action adequate for the demands of the time. The restricted strike is today losing more and more of its original importance, even if it is not doomed to disappear altogether. In the modern economic struggle between capital and labour the big strike, involving entire industries, will play a larger and larger part. Even the workers in the old craft organisations, which are as yet untouched by Socialist ideas, have grasped that, as is shown clearly enough by the rapid springing up of industrial unions in America in contrast with the old methods of the A.F.of L.

Direct action by organised labour finds its strongest expression in the general strike, in the stoppage of work in every branch of production by the organised resistance of the proletariat, with all the consequences arising from it. It is the most powerful weapon which the workers have at their command, and gives the most comprehensive expression to their strength as a social factor. After the French trade union congress in Marseilles (1892), and the later congresses of the C.G.T. (General Federation of Labour) had by a large majority declared for the propaganda of the general strike, it was the political labour parties in Germany and most other countries which assailed most violently this form of proletarian action, and rejected it as "Utopian." "The general strike is general madness" was the trenchant phrase which was coined at that time by one of the most prominent leaders of the German Social Democracy. But the great strike movement of the years immediately following, in Spain, Belgium, Italy, Holland, Russia, and so on, showed clearly that this alleged "Utopia" lay wholly within the realm of the possible and did not arise from the imagination of a few revolutionary fanatics.

The general strike is, of course, not an agency that can be invoked arbitrarily on every occasion. It needs certain social assumptions to give it its proper moral strength and make it a proclamation of the will of the broad masses of the people. The ridiculous claim, which is so often attributed to the Anarcho-Syndicalists, that it is only necessary to proclaim a general strike in order to achieve a Socialist society in a few days, is, of course, just a silly invention of evil-minded opponents bent on discrediting an idea which they cannot attack by any other means.

The general strike can serve various purposes. It can be the last stage of a sympathetic strike, as for example, the general strike in Barcelona in February, 1902, or that in Bilbao in October, 1903, which enabled the mine workers to get rid of the hated truck system and compelled the employers to establish sanitary conditions on the mines. It can as easily be a means by which organised labour tries to enforce some general demand, as, for example, in the attempted general strike in the U.S.A. in 1886, to compel the granting of the eight-hour day in all industries. The great general strike of the English workers in 1926 was the result of a planned attempt by the employers to lower the general standard of living of the workers by a cut in wages.

But the general strike can also have political objectives in view, as, for example, the fight of the Spanish workers in 1904, for the liberation of political prisoners, or the general strike in Catalonia in July, 1909, to compel the government to terminate the war in Morocco. And the general strike of the German workers in 1920, which was instituted after the so-called Kapp putsch and put an end to a government that had attained to power by a military uprising, belongs to this category; as do also the mass strikes in Belgium in 1903, and in Sweden in 1909, to compel the granting of universal suffrage, and the general strike of the Russian workers in 1905, for the granting of the constitution. But in Spain the widespread strike movement among the workers and peasants after the Fascist revolt in July, 1936, developed into a "social general strike" (huelga general) and led to armed resistance, and with this to the abolishment of the capitalist economic order and the reorganisation of the economic life by the workers themselves.

The great importance of the general strike lies in this: at one blow it brings the whole economic system to a standstill and shakes it to its foundations. Moreover, such an action is in no wise dependent on the practical preparedness of all the workers, as all the citizens of a country have never participated in a social overturn. That the organised workers in the most important industries quit work is enough to cripple the entire economic mechanism, which cannot function without the daily provision of coal, electric power, and raw materials of every sort. But when the ruling classes are confronted with an energetic, organised working class, schooled in daily conflict, and are aware of what they have at stake, they become much more willing to make the necessary concessions, and, above all, they fear to take a course with the workers which might drive them to extremes. Even Jean Jaurès who, as a Socialist parliamentarian, was not in agreement with the idea of the general strike, had to concede that the constant danger arising from the possibility of such a movement admonished the possessing classes to caution, and, above everything, made them shrink from the suppression of hard-won rights, since they saw that this could easily lead to catastrophe.

But at the time of a universal social crisis, or when, as today in Spain, the concern is to protect an entire people against the attacks of benighted reactionaries, the general strike is an invaluable weapon, for which there is no substitute. By crippling the whole public life it makes difficult mutual agreements of the representatives of the ruling classes and the local officials with the central government, even when it does not entirely prevent them. Even the use of the army is, in such cases, directed at very different tasks from those of political revolt. In the latter case it suffices for the government, so long as it can rely on the military, to concentrate its troops in the capital and the most important points in the country, in order to meet the danger that threatens.

A general strike, however, leads inevitably to a scattering of the military forces, as in such a situation the important concern is the protection of all important centres of industry and the transport system against the rebellious workers. But this means that military discipline, which is always strongest when soldiers operate in fixed formations, is relaxed. Where the military in small groups faces a determined people fighting for its freedom, there always exists the possibility that at least a part of the soldiers will reach some inner insight and comprehend that, after all, it is their own parents and brothers at whom they are pointing their weapons. For militarism, also, is primarily a psychologic problem, and its disastrous influence always manifests itself where the individual is given no chance to think about his dignity as a human being, no chance to see that there are higher tasks in life than lending oneself to the uses of a bloody oppressor of one's own people.

For the workers the general strike takes the place of the barricades of the political uprising. It is for them a logical outcome of the industrial system whose victims they are today, and at the same time it offers them their strongest weapon in their struggle for liberation, provided they recognise their own strength and learn how to use this weapon properly. William Morris, with the prophetic vision of the poet, foresaw this development in affair, when, in his splendid book *News from Nowhere*, he has the Socialist reconstruction of society preceded by a long series of general strikes of ever increasing violence, which shook the old system to its deepest foundations, until at last its supporters were no longer able to put up any resistance against this new enlightenment of the toiling masses in town and country.

The whole development of modern capitalism, which is today growing into an ever graver danger to society, can but serve to spread this enlightenment more widely among the workers. The fruitlessness of the participation of the organised workers in parliaments, which is today becoming more and more manifest in every country, of itself compels them to look about for new methods for the effective defence of their interests and their eventual liberation from the yoke of wage slavery.

Another important fighting device for direct action is the boycott. It can be employed by the workers both in their character of producers and of consumers. A systematic refusal of consumers to buy from firms that handle goods not produced under conditions approved by the labour unions can often be of decisive importance, especially for those branches of labour engaged in the production of commodities of general use. At the same time the boycott is very well adapted to influencing public opinion in favour of the workers, provided it is accompanied by suitable propaganda. The union label is a effective means of facilitating the boycott, at it gives the purchaser the sign by which to distinguish the goods he wants from the spurious. Even the masters of the Third Reich experienced what a weapon the boycott can become in the hands of the great masses of people, when they had to confess that the international boycott against German goods had inflicted serious damage on German export trade. And this influence might have been greater still, if the trade unions had kept public opinion alert by incessant propaganda, and had continued to foster the protest against the suppression of the German labour movement.

As producers the boycott provides the workers with the means of imposing an embargo on individual plants whose managers show themselves especially hostile to trade unions. In Barcelona, Valencia and Cadiz the refusal of the longshoremen to unload German vessels compelled the captains of these vessels to discharge their cargoes in North African harbours. If the trade unions in the other countries had resolved on the same procedure, they would have achieved incomparably greater results than by Platonic protests. In any case the boycott is one of the most effective fighting devices in the hands of the working class, and the more profoundly aware of this device the workers become, the more comprehensive and successful will they become in their everyday struggles.

Among the weapons in the Anarcho-Syndicalist armoury *sabotage* is the one most feared by the employer and most harshly condemned as "unlawful." In realty we are dealing here with a method of economic petty warfare that is as old as the system of exploitation and political oppression itself. It is, in some circumstances, simply forced upon the workers, when every other device fails. Sabotage consists in the workers putting every possible obstacle in the way of the ordinary modes of work. For the most part this occurs when the employers try to avail themselves of a bad economic situation or some other favourable occasion to lower the normal conditions of labour by curtailment of wages or by lengthening of the hours of labour. The term itself is derived from the French word, *sabot*, wooden shoe, and means *to work clumsily as if by sabot blows*. The whole import of sabotage is exhausted in the motto: for bad wages, bad work. The employer himself acts on the same principle, when he calculates the price of his goods according to their quality. The producer finds himself in the same position: his goods are his labour-power, and it is only good and proper that he should try to dispose of it on the best terms he can get.

But when the employer takes advantage of the evil position of the producer to force the price of his labour-power as low as possible, he need not wonder when the latter defends himself as best he can and for this purpose makes use of the means which the circumstances put in his hands. The English workers were already doing this long before revolutionary Syndicalism was spoken of on the continent. In fact the policy of "*ca' canny*" (go slow), which, along with the phrase itself, the English workers took over from their Scottish brethren, was the first and most effective form of sabotage. There are today in every industry a hundred means by which the workers can seriously disturb production; everywhere under the modern system of division of labour, where often the slightest disturbance in one branch of the work can bring to a standstill the entire process of production. Thus the railway workers in France and Italy by the use of the so-called *grève perlée* (string-of-pearls-strike) threw the whole system of transportation into disorder. For this they needed to do nothing more than to adhere to the strict letter of the existing transport laws, and thus made it impossible for any train to arrive at its destination on time. When the employers are at once faced with the fact that even in an unfavourable situation, where the workers would not dare to think of a strike, they still have in their hands the means of defending themselves, there will also come to them the understanding that it does not pay to make use of some particular hard situation of the workers of force harder conditions of living upon them.

The so-called *sit down strike*, which was transplanted from Europe to America with such suprising rapidity and consists of the workers remaining in the plant day and night without turning a finger in order to prevent the installing of strike-breakers, belongs in the realm of sabotage. Very often sabotage works thus: before a strike the workers put the machines out of order to make the work of possible strike-breakers harder, or even impossible for a considerable time. In no field is there as so much scope for the imagination of the worker as in this. But the sabotage of the workers is directed against the employers, never against the consumers. In his report before the C.G.T. in Toulouse in 1897, Emile Pouget laid special stress on this point. All the reports in the bourgeois press about bakers who had baked glass in their bread, or farm hands who had poisoned milk, and the like, are malicious inventions, designed solely to prejudice the public against the workers.

Sabotaging the consumers is the age old-privilege of the employers. The deliberate adulteration of provisions, the construction of wretched slums and insanitary tenements of the poorest and cheapest material, the destruction of great quantities of foodstuffs in order to keep up prices, while millions are perishing in direst misery, the constant efforts of the employers to force the subsistence of the workers down to the lowest point possible, in order to grab for themselves the highest possible profits, the shameless practice of the armament industries of supplying foreign countries with complete equipment for war, which, given the appropriate occasion, may be employed to lay waste the country that produced them, all these and many more are merely individual items in an interminable list of types of sabotage by capitalists against their own people.

Another form of direct action is the *social strike*, which will, without doubt, in the immediate future play a much larger part. It is concerned less with the immediate interests of the producers than with the protection of the community against the most pernicious outgrowths of the present system. The social strike seeks to force upon the employers a responsibility to the public. Primarily it has in view the protection of the consumers, of whom the workers themselves constitute the great majority. The task of the trade union has heretofore been restricted almost exclusively to the protection of the worker as producer. As long as the employer was observing the hours of labour agreed on and paying the established wage this task was being performed. In other words: *the trade union is interested only in the conditions under which its members work, not in the kind of work they perform.* Theoretically, it is, indeed, asserted that the relation between employer and employee is based upon a contract for the accomplishment of a definite purpose. The purpose in this case is social production. But a contract has meaning only when both parties participate equally in the purpose. In reality, however, the worker has today no voice in determining production, for this is given over completely to the employer. The consequence is that the worker is debased by doing a thousand things which constantly serve only to injure the whole community for the advantage of the employer. He is compelled to make use of inferior and often actually injurious materials in the fabrication of his products, to erect wretched dwellings, to put up spoiled foodstuffs, and to perpetuate innumerable acts that are planned to cheat the consumer.

To interfere vigorously here is, in the opinion of the Anarcho-Syndicalists, the great task of the trade unions of the future. An advance in this direction would at the same time enhance the position of the workers in society, and in large measure confirm that position. Various efforts in this field have already been made, as witness, for example, the strike of the building-workers in Barcelona, who refused to use poor material and the wreckage from old buildings in the erection of workers' dwelling (1902), the strikes in various large restaurants in Paris because the kitchen workers were unwilling to prepare for serving cheap, decaying meat (1906), and a long list of instances in recent times; all going to prove that the workers' understanding of their responsibility to society is growing. The resolution of the German armament workers at the congress in Erfurt (1919) to make no more weapons of war and to compel their employers to convert their plants to other uses, belongs also to this category. And it is a fact that this resolution was maintained for almost two years, until it was broken by the Central Trades Unions. The Anarcho-Syndicalist workers of Sommerda resisted with great energy to the last, when their place were taken by members of the "free labour unions."

As outspoken opponents of all nationalist ambitions the revolutionary Syndicalists, especially in the Latin countries, have always devoted a very considerable part of their activity to anti-militarist propaganda, seeking to hold the workers in soldiers' coats loyal to their class and to prevent their turning their weapons against their brethren in time of a strike. This has cost them great sacrifices; but they have never ceased their efforts, because they know that they can regain their efforts only by incessant warfare against the dominant powers. At the same time, however, the anti-militarist propaganda contributes in large measure to oppose the threat of wars to come with the general strike. The Anarcho-Syndicalists know that wars are only waged in the interest of the ruling classes; they believe, therefore, that any means is justifiable that can prevent the organised murder of peoples. In this field also the workers have every means in their hands, if only they possess the desire and the moral strength to use them.

Above all it is necessary to cure the labour movement of its inner ossification and rid it of the empty sloganeering of the political parties, so that it may forge ahead intellectually and develop within itself the creative conditions which must precede the realisation of Socialism. The practical attainability of this goal must become for the workers an inner certainty and must ripen into an ethical necessity. The great final goal of Socialism must emerge from all the practical daily struggles, and must give them a social character. In the pettiest struggle, born of the needs of the moment, there must be mirrored the great goal of social liberation, and each such struggle must help to smooth the way and strengthen the spirit which transforms the inner longing of its bearers into will and deed.

Chapter 6. The Evolution of Anarcho-Syndicalism

Revolutionary Syndicalism in France and its Influence on the labour movement in Europe; The Industrial Workers of the World; Syndicalism after the First World War; The Syndicalists and the Third International; The founding of the new International Workingmen's Association; Anarcho-Syndicalism in Spain; In Portugal; In Italy; In France; In Germany; In Sweden; In Holland; In South America.

The modern Anarcho-Syndicalist movement in Europe, with the single exception of Spain where from the days of the First International Anarcho-Syndicalism has always been the dominant tendency in the labour movement, owes its origin to the rise of revolutionary Syndicalism in France, with its field of influence in the C.G.T. This movement developed quite spontaneously within the French working class as a reaction against political Socialism, the cleavages in which for a long time permitted no unified trade union movement. After the fall of the Paris Commune and the outlawing of the International in France the labour movement there had taken on a completely colourless character and had fallen completely under the influence of the bourgeois Republican, J. Barberet, whose slogan was: "Harmony between capital and labour!" Not until the congress in Marseilles (1879) did any Socialist tendencies again manifest themselves and the *Fédération des Travailleurs* came into being, itself to come quickly and completely under the influence of the so-called collectivists.

But even the collectivists did not long remain united, and the congress of St. Etienne (1882) brought a split in this movement. One section followed the school of the Marxist, Jules Guesde, and founded the *Parti Ouvrie Français*, while the other section attached itself to the former Anarchist, Paul Brousse, to form the *Parti Ouvrier Révolutionare Socialiste Français*. The former found its support chiefly in the Fédération Nationale des Syndicats, while the latter had its stronghold in the Fédération des Bourses du Travail de France (Federation of Labour Exchanges of France). After a short time the so-called Allemanists, under the leadership of Jean Alleman, broke away from the Broussists and attained a powerful influence in some of the large syndicates; they had given up parliamentary activity completely. Besides these there were the Blanquists, united in the *Comité Révolutionaire Central*, and the independent Socialists, who belonged to the *Société pour L'Economie Sociale*, which had been founded in 1885 by Benoit Malon, and out of which came both Jean Jaurès and Millerand.

All of these parties, with the exception of the Allemanists, saw in the trade unions merely recruiting schools for their political objectives, and had no understanding whatever of their real functions. The constant dissension among the various Socialist factions were naturally carried over to the syndicats, with the results that when the trade unions of one faction went on strike, the syndicats of the other factions walked in on them as strike-breakers. This untenable situation gradually opened the eyes of the workers eyes, on awakening to which the anti-parliamentary propaganda of the Anarchists, who since 1883 had a strong following among the workers in Paris and Lyons, contributed not a little. So the Trade Union Congress at Nantes (1894) charged a special committee with the task of devising ways and means for bringing about an understanding among all the trade union alliances. The result was the founding in the following year at the Congress in Limonges, of the C.G.T., which declared itself independent of all political parties. It was the final renunciation by the trade unions of political Socialism, whose operations had crippled the French labour movement and deprived it of its most effective weapon in the fight for liberation.

From there on there existed only two large trade union groups, the C.G.T. and the Federation of Labour Exchanges, until in 1902, at the Congress of Montpellier the latter joined the C.N.T. With this there was brought about practical unity of the trade unions. This effort at the unification of organised labour was preceded by an intensive propaganda for the general strike, for which the congresses at Marseilles (1892), Paris (1893), and Nantes (1894) had already declared by strong majorities. The idea of the general strike was first brought into the trade union movement by the Anarchist carpenter, Tortelier, who had been deeply stirred by the general strike movement on the U.S.A. in 1886–7, and it had been later taken up by the Allemanists, while Jules Guesde and the French Marxists had emphatically pronounced against it. However, both movements furnished the C.N.T. with a lot of its most distinguished representatives: from the Allemanists came, in particular, V. Griffuelles; from the Anarchists, F. Pelloutier, the devoted and highly intelligent secretary of the Federation of Labour Exchanges, E. Pouget, editor of the official organ of the C.G.T., *La Voix du Peuple*, P. Delesalle, G. Yvetot, and many others. One often encounters in other countries, the widely disseminated opinion, which was fostered by Werner Sombart in particular, that revolutionary Syndicalism in France owes its origin to intellectuals like G. Sorel, E. Berth and H. Lagardelle, who in the periodical, *Le Mouvement Socialiste*, founded it 1899, elaborated in their own way the intellectual results of the new movement. This is utterly false. These men never belonged to the movement themselves, nor had they any mentionable influence on its internal development. Moreover, the C.G.T. was not composed exclusively of revolutionary trade unions, certainly half of its members were of reformist tendency and had only joined the C.G.T. because they recognised that the dependence of the trade unions on the political parties was a misfortune for the movement. But the revolutionary wing, which had the most energetic and active elements in organised labour on its side and had at its command, moreover, the best intellectual forces in the organisation, gave to the C.G.T. its characteristic stamp, and it was they, exclusively, who determined the development of the ideas of revolutionary Syndicalism.

With it the ideas of the old International wakened to new life, and there was initiated that storm-and-stress period of the French labour movement, whose revolutionary influences made themselves felt far beyond the boundaries of France. The great strike movements and the countless prosecutions of the C.G.T. by the government merely strengthened their revolutionary verve, and caused the new ideas to find their way also into Switzerland, Germany, Italy, Holland, Belgium, Bohemia, and the Scandinavian counties. In England also the *Syndicalist Education League*, which had been brought into existence in 1910 by Tom Mann and Guy Bowman, and whose teachings exercised a very strong influence, especially among the rank-and-file of the transport and mining industries, as was revealed in the great strike movements of that period, owed its existence to French Syndicalism.

The influence of French Syndicalism on the international labour movement was strengthened in great degree by the internal crisis which at that time laid hold of nearly all the Socialist labour parties. The battle between the so-called Revisionists and the rigid Marxists, and particularly the fact that their very parliamentary activities forced the most violent opponents of revisionism of natural necessity to travel in practise the revisionary path, caused many of the more thoughtful element to reflect seriously. Thus it came about that most of the parties found themselves driven by the force of circumstances, often against their will, to make certain concessions to the general strike idea of the Syndicalists. Before this Domela Nieuwenhuis, the pioneer of the Socialist labour movement in Holland, had brought up in the International Congress of Socialists in Brussels (1891) a proposal for warding off the approaching danger of a war by preparing organised labour for the general strike, a proposal which was most bitterly opposed by Wilhelm Liebknect in particular. But in spite of this opposition almost all national and international Socialist congresses were subsequently obliged to concern themselves more and more with this question.

At the Socialist congress in Paris in 1899, the future minister, Aristide Briand, argued for the general strike with all his fiery eloquence and succeeded in having an appropriate resolution adopted by the congress. Even the French Guesdists, who had previously been the bitterest foes of the general strike, found themselves obliged at the congress in Lille (1904) to adopt a resolution favouring it, as they feared they would otherwise lose all their influence with the workers. Of course nothing was gained by such concessions. The see-saw back and forth between parliamentarism and direct action could only cause confusion. Straightforward men like Domela Nieuwenhuis and his followers in Holland, and the Allemanists in France, drew the inevitable inference from their new conception of things and withdrew entirely from parliamentary activity; for the others, however, their concessions to the idea of the general strike were merely lip service, with no clear understanding behind it. Whither that led was shown nicely in the case of Briand, who, as a minister, found himself in the tragic-comic situation of being obliged to prohibit his own address in favour of the general strike, which the C.G.T. had distributed in pamphlet form by the hundred thousand.

Independent of European Syndicalism there developed in the U.S.A. the movement of the *Industrial Workers of the World*, which was wholly the outgrowth of American conditions. Still it had in common with Syndicalism the methods of direct action and the idea of a Socialist reorganisation of society by the industrial and agricultural organisation of the workers themselves. At its founding congress in Chicago (1905) the most diverse radical elements in the American labour movement were represented: Eugene Debs, Bill Haywood, Charles Moyer, Daniel De Leon, W. Trautmann, Mother Jones, Lucy Parsons and many others. The most important section for a time was the *Western Federation of Miners* whose name was known everywhere for its devoted and self-sacrificing labour fights in Colorado, Montana and Idaho. Since the great movement for the eight-hour day in 1886-7, which came to its tragic conclusion with the execution of the Anarchists, Spies, Parsons, Fletcher. Engel and Lingg on November 11, 1877, the American labour movement had been completely bogged down spiritually. It was believed that by the founding of the I.W.W. it might be possible to put the movement back on its revolutionary course, an expectation which has thus far not been fulfilled. What chiefly distinguished the I.W.W. from the European Syndicalists was its strongly defined Marxist views, which were impressed on it more particularly by Daniel De Leon while European Syndicalists had conspicuously adopted the Socialist ideas of the libertarian wing of the First International.

The I.W.W. had an especially strong influence on the itinerant workers in the West, but they also gained some influence among factory workers in the eastern states, and conducted a great many wide-spread strikes, which put the name of the "Wobblies" in everybody's mouth. They took an outstanding part in the embittered battles for the safeguarding of freedom of speech in the Western states, and made many terrible sacrifices of life and liberty in doing so. Their members filled the jails by thousands, many were tarred and feathered by fanatical vigilantes, or lynched outright. The Everett massacre of 1916, the execution of the labour poet, Joe Hill, in 1915, the Centralia affair in 1919, and a lot of similar cases in which defenceless workers fell victims, were only a few mile stones in the I.W.W.'s history of sacrifice.

The outbreak of the World War affected the labour movement like a natural catastrophe of enormous scope. After the assassinations at Sarajevo, when everybody felt that Europe was driving under full sail toward a general war, the leaders of the C.G.T. proposed to the leaders of the German trade unions that organised labour in the two countries should take joint action to halt the threatened disaster. But the German labour leaders, who always opposed any direct mass action, and in their long years of parliamentary routine had long since lost every trace of revolutionary initiative, could not be won over to such a proposal. So failed the last chance for preventing the frightful catastrophe.

After the war the peoples faced a new situation. Europe was bleeding from a thousand wounds and writhing as if in the throes of a fever. In Central Europe the old regime had collapsed. Russia found herself in the midst of a social revolution of which no one could see the end. Of all the events after the war the occurrences in Russia had impressed the workers in every country most deeply. They felt instinctively that they were in the midst of a revolutionary situation, and that, if nothing decisive came out of it now, all the hopes of the toiling masses would be dispelled for years. The workers recognised that the system which had been unable to prevent the horrible catastrophe of the World War, but instead for four years had driven the peoples to the slaughter-pen, had forfeited its right to existence, and they hailed any effort which promised them a way out of the economic and political chaos which the war had created. For just this reason they placed their highest hopes on the Russian revolution and thought it marked the inauguration of a new era in the history of the European peoples.

In 1919 the Bolshevist party, which had attained to power in Russia, issued an appeal to the revolutionary workers' organisations in the world, and invited them to a congress which was to meet in Russia in the following year to set up a new International. Communist parties exist at that time in only a few countries; on the other hand, there were in Spain, Portugal, Italy, France, Holland, Sweden, Germany, England and the countries of North and South America Syndicalist organisations, some of which exercised a very strong influence. It was, therefore, of deep concern to Lenin and his followers to win these particular organisations, as he had so thoroughly alienated himself from the Socialist labour parties that he could scarcely count upon their support. So it came about that, at the congress for the founding of the Third International in the summer of 1920, almost all of the Syndicalist and Anarcho-Syndicalist organisations were represented.

But the impressions which the Syndicalist delegates received in Russia were not calculated to make them regard collaboration with the Communists as either possible or desirable. The "dictatorship of the proletariat" was already revealing itself in its worst light. The prisons were filled with Socialists of every school, among them many Anarchists and Anarcho-Syndicalists. But above all it was plain that the new dominant caste was in no way fitted for the task of genuine Socialist reconstruction.

The foundation of the Third International, with its dictatorial apparatus of organisation and its effort to make the whole labour movement of Europe into an instrument of the foreign policy of the Bolshevist state, quickly made plain to the Syndicalists that there was no place for them in that organisation. But it was very necessary for the Bolshevists, and Lenin in particular, to establish a hold on the syndicalist organisation abroad, as their importance, especially in the Latin countries, was well known. For this reason it was decided to set up, alongside the Third International, a separate international alliance of all revolutionary trade unions, in which the Syndicalist organisations of all shades could also find a place. The Syndicalist delegates agreed to the proposal and began negotiations with Losovsky, the commissioner of the Communist International. But he demanded that the new organisation should be subordinate to the Third International, and that the Syndicates in the several countries should be placed under the leadership of the Communist organisations in their countries. This demand was unanimously rejected by the Syndicalist delegates. As they were unable to come to an agreement on any terms, it was at last decided to hold and international trade union congress in Moscow the following year, 1921, and to leave the decision of his question to it.

In December, 1920, an international Syndicalist conference convened in Berlin to decide upon an attitude toward the approaching congress in Moscow. The congress agreed upon seven points, on the acceptance of which their entrance into the Red Trade Union International was made dependent. The most important of these seven points was the complete independence of the movement from all political parties, and insistence on the viewpoint that the Socialist reorganisation of society could only be carried out by the economic organisations of the producing classes themselves. At the congress in Moscow in the following year the Syndicalist organisations were in the minority. The *Central Alliance of Russian Trade Unions* dominated the entire situation and put through all the resolutions.

In conjunction with the thirteenth congress of the F.A.U.D. (*Freie Arbeiter-Union Deutschlands*, Free Labour Union of Germany) at Düsseldorf in October, 1921, there was held an international organisation of Syndicalist organisations at which delegates from Germany, Sweden, Holland, Czechoslovakia and the I.W.W. in America were present. The conference voted for the calling of an international Syndicalist congress in the spring of 1922. Berlin was selected as the meeting place. In July, 1922, a conference was held in Berlin to make preparations for this congress; France, Germany, Norway, Sweden, Holland, Spain and the revolutionary Syndicalists in Russia were represented. The Central Alliance of Russian Trade Unions had also sent a delegate who did his best to prevent the calling of the congress, and when he had no success in this left the congress. The conference worked out a declaration of the principles of revolutionary Syndicalism, which was to be laid before the coming congress for consideration, and made all the necessary preparations for making the congress a success.

The International Congress of Syndicalists met in Berlin from December 25, 1922, until January 2, 1923, the following organisations being represented; Argentina by the *Federaction Obrera Regional Argentina*, with 200,000 members; Chile by the *Industrial Workers of the World*, with 20,000 members; Denmark by the *Union for Syndicalist Propaganda*, with 600 members; Germany by the *Freie Arbeiter-Union*, with 120,000 members; Holland by the *National Arbeids Sekretariat*, with 22,500 members; Italy by the *Unione Sindicale Italiana*, 500,000 members; Mexico by the *Confederación General de Trabajadores*, with 30,000 members; Norway by the *Norsk Syndikalistik Federasjon*, with 20,000 members; Portugal by the *Confederaçao Geral do Trabalho*, with 150,000 members; Sweden by the *Sveriges Arbetares Centralorganisation*, with 32,000 members. The Spanish C.N.T. was at that time engaged in a terrific struggle against the dictatorship of Primo de Rivera, and for that reason had sent no delegate, but they reaffirmed their adherence at the secret conference in Saragossa in October, 1923. In France, where after the war a split in the C.G.T. had taken place, leading to the founding of the C.G.T.U., the latter had already joined the Muscovites. But there was a minority in the organisation which had combined to form the *Comité de Défence Syndicaliste Revolutionaire*. This committee, which represented about 100,000 workers, took active part in the proceedings of the Berlin congress. From France the Federation des feunesses de la Seine were likewise represented. Two delegates represented the Syndicalist minority of the Russian trade unions.

The congress resolved unanimously on the founding of an international alliance of all Syndicalist organisations under the name *International Workingmen's Association*. It adopted the declaration of principles that had been worked out by the Berlin preliminary conference, which presented an outspoken profession of Anarcho-Syndicalism. The second item on this declaration runs as follows:

> "Revolutionary Syndicalism is the confirmed enemy of every form of economic and social monopoly, and aims at its abolition by means of economic communes and administrative organs of field and factory workers on the basis of a free system of councils, entirely liberated from subordination to any government or political party. Against the politics of the state and of parties it erects the economic organisation of labour; against the government of men, it sets up the administration of things. Consequently, it has for its object not the conquest of political power, but the abolition of every State function in social life. It considers that, along with the monopoly of property, should disappear also the monopoly of domination, and that any form of the State, including the dictatorship of the proletariat, will always be the creator of new privileges; it could never be an instrument of liberation."

With this the breach with Bolshevism and its adherents in the separate countries was completed. The I.W.M.A. from then on travelled its own road and gained a foothold in a number of countries which had not been represented at the founding congress. It holds its international congresses, issues its bulletins, and adjusts the relations between the Syndicalists organisations of the different countries. Among all the international alliances of organised labour it is the one that has most faithfully cherished the traditions of the First International.

The most powerful and influential organisation in the I.W.M.A. is the Spanish C.N.T., which is making history in Europe today and is, moreover, discharging one of the hardest tasks that has ever been set before the workers' organisation. The C.N.T. was founded in 1910, and within a few years counted as members over a million workers and peasants. The organisation was new only in name, not in objectives or methods. The history of the Spanish labour movement is shot through with long periods of reaction, in which the movement has been able to carry on only an underground existence. But after every such period it has organised anew. The name changes, but the goal remains the same. The labour movement in Spain goes back to 1840, when the weaver, Juan Munts, in Catalonia, brought into being in Barcelona the first trade union of textile workers. The government of that day sent General Zapatero to Catalonia to put down the movement. The consequence was the great general strike of 1855, which led to an open revolt in which the workers inscribed on their banners the slogan: *Associación ó Muerte!* (The right to organise or death!) The rebellion was bloodily suppressed, but the government granted the workers the right of organisation.

The first movement of the Spanish workers was strongly influenced by the ideas of Pi y Margall, leader of the Spanish Federalists and disciple of Proudhon. Pi y Margall was one of the outstanding theorists of his time and had a powerful influence on the development of libertarian ideas in Spain. His political ideas had much in common with those of Richard Price, Joseph Priestly, Thomas Paine, Jefferson, and other representatives of the Anglo-American liberalism of the first period. He wanted to limit the power of the state to a minimum and gradually replace it by a Socialist economic order. In 1868, after the abdication of King Amadeo I, Bakunin addressed his celebrated manifest to the Spanish workers, and sent a special delegation to Spain to win the workers to the First International. Tens of thousands of workers joined the great workers' alliance and adopted the Anarcho-Syndicalist ideas of Bakunin, to which they have remained loyal to this day. As a matter of fact, the Spanish Federation was the strongest organisation in the International. After the overthrow of the first Spanish republic the International was suppressed in Spain, but it continued to exist as an underground movement, issued its periodicals, and bade defiance to every tyranny. And when, finally, after seven years of unheard-of persecution, the exceptional law against the workers was repealed, there immediately sprang to life the *Federaction de Trabajadores de la Región Española*, at whose second congress in Sevilla (1882) there were already represented 218 local federations with 70,000 members.

No other workers' organisation in the world has had to endure such frightful persecution as the Anarchist labour movement in Spain. Hundreds of its adherents were executed or horrible tortured by inhuman inquisitors in the prisons of Jerez de la Forntera, Montjuich, Sevilla, Alcalá del Valle, and so on. The bloody persecutions of the so-called *Mano Negra* (Black Hand), which actually never existed, was a pure invention of the government to justify the suppression of the organisations of the field workers in Andalusia; the gruesome tragedy of Montjuich, which in its day roused a storm of protest from the entire world; the acts of terrorism of the of the *Camisas Blancas* (White Shirts), a gangster organisation which had been brought into existence by the police and the employers to clear away the leaders of the movement by assassination, and to which even the General Secretary of the C.N.T., Salvador Segui, fell victim — these are just a few chapters in the long, torture-filled story of the Spanish labour movement. Fransisco Ferrer, founder of the Modern School in Barcelona and publisher of the paper *La Huelga General* (The General Strike) was one of its martyrs. But no reaction was ever able to crush the resistance of its adherents. That movement has produced hundreds of the most marvellous characters, whose purity of heart and inflexible idealism had to be acknowledged even by their grimmest opponents. The Spanish Anarchist labour movement had no place for political careerists. What it had to offer was constant danger, imprisonment, and often death. Only when one has become acquainted with the frightful story of the martyrs of this movement does one understand why it has assumed at certain periods such a violent character in defence of its human rights against the onslaughts of black reactionaries.

The present C.N.T.-F.A.I. embodies the old traditions of the movement. In contrast with the Anarchists of many other countries, their comrades in Spain from the beginning based their activities on the economic fighting organisations of the workers. The C.N.T. today embraces a membership of two and a half million workers and peasants. It controls thirty-six daily papers, among them *Solidaredad Obrera* in Barcelona, with a circulation of 240,000, the largest of any paper in Spain, and *Castilla Libre*, which is the most read paper in Madrid. Besides these the movements put out a lot of weekly publications and possesses six of the best reviews in the country. During the last year, in particular, it has published a large number of excellent books and pamphlets and has contributed more to the education of the masses than has any other movement. The C.N.T.-F.A.I. is, today, the backbone of the heroic struggle against Fascism in Spain and the soul of the social reorganisation of the country.

In Portugal, where the labour movement has always been strongly influenced by neighbouring Spain, there was formed in 1911 the *Confederacçao Geral do Trabalho*, the strongest workers' organisation in the country, representing the same principles as the C.N.T. in Spain. It has always sharply its independence of all political parties, and had conducted a lot of big strike movements. By the victory of the dictatorship in Portugal the C.G.T. was forced out of political activity and today leads an underground existence. The recent disturbances in Portugal, directed against the existing reaction, are chiefly traceable to its activities.

In Italy there always existed, from the days of the First International, a strong Anarchist movement which, in certain sections of the country retained a decisive influence over the workers and peasants. In 1902 the Socialist Party founded the *Confederazione del Lavoro*, which was patterned after the model of the German trade union organisations of the country. But it never attained this goal; it was not even able to prevent a large part of its membership from being strongly influenced by the ideas of the French Syndicalists. A few big and successful strikes, especially the farmlabourers' strike in Parma and Ferrara, gave a strong impetus to the prestige of the advocates of direct action. In 1912 there convened in Modena a conference of various organisations which were not at all in accord with the method of the Confederation and its subservience to the influence of the Socialist Party. This conference formed a new organisation under the name *Unione Sindicale Italiana*. This body was the soul of a long list of labour struggles op to the outbreak of the World War. In particular it took a prominent part in the occurrences of the so-called *Red Week* in June, 1913. The brutal attacks of the police on striking workers in Ancona led to general strike, which in a few provinces developed into an armed insurrection.

When, in following year, the World War broke out, a serious crisis arose in the U.S.I. The most influential leader of the movement, Alceste de Ambris, who had all the time played a rather ambiguous role, tried to rouse in the organisation a sentiment for the war. At the congress in Parma (1914), however, he found himself in the minority, and, with his followers, withdrew from the movement. Upon Italy's entrance into the war all the known propagandists of the U.S.I. were arrested and imprisoned until the end of the war. After the war a revolutionary situation arose in Italy, and the events in Russia, whose actual significance could at that time, of course, not be foreseen, roused a vigorous response in the country. The U.S.I. in a short time awoke to new life and soon counted 600,000 members. A series of serious labour disturbances shook the country, reaching their peak in the occupation of the factories in August, 1920. Its goal at that time was a free soviet system, which was to reject any dictatorship and find its basis in the economic organisations of organised labour.

In that same year, the U.S.I. sent its secretary, Armando Borghi, to Moscow to acquaint himself personally with the situation in Russia. Borghi returned to Italy sadly disillusioned. In the interim the Communists had been trying to get the U.S.I. into their hands; but the congress at Rome in 1922 led to an open break with Bolshevism and the affiliation of the organisation with the I.W.M.A. Meanwhile Fascism had developed into an immediate danger. A strong and united labour movement that was determined to risk everything in defence of its freedom could still have put a check upon this danger. But the pitiful conduct of the Socialist Party and the Confederation of Labour, which was subject to its influence, wrecked everything. Besides the U.S.I. there remained only the only the *Unione Anarchia Italiana* to rally round the universally revered champion of Italian Anarchism, Errico Malatesta. When in 1922 the general strike against Fascism broke out, the democratic government armed the Fascist hordes and throttled this last attempt at the defence of freedom and right. But Italian democracy had dug its own grave. It thought it could use Mussolini as a tool against the workers, but thus it became its own grave-digger. With the victory of Fascism the whole Italian labour movement disappeared, and along with it the U.S.I. and all openness in social life.

In France after the war the so-called reformist wing had gained the upper-hand in the C.G.T., whereupon the revolutionary elements seceded and formed themselves into the C.G.T.U. But since Moscow had a very strong interest in getting this particular organisation into its hands, there was started in it an unscrupulous underground activity in cells after the Russian pattern which went so far that in 1922 two Anarcho-Syndicalists were shot down by Communists in the Paris Trade Union house. Thereupon the Anarcho-Syndicalists, with Pierre Bernard, withdrew from the C.G.T.U., and formed the *Confédération Générale du Travail Syndicaliste Revolutionaire*, which joined the International Workingmens' Association. This organisation has since then been vigorously active and has contributed greatly to keep alive among the workers the old pre-war ideas of the C.G.T. The disillusionment over Russia and, above all, the resounding echo amongst the French workers of the Spanish fight for freedom, led to a strong revival of revolutionary Syndicalism in France, so that one can safely count on a rebirth of the movement within predictable time.

In Germany there had existed for a long time before the war the movement of the so-called *Localists*, whose stronghold was the *Freie Vereigung deutscher Gewerkschaften*, founded by G.Kessler and F. Kater in 1897. This organisation was originally inspired by purely Social Democratic ideas, but it combated the centralising tendencies of the general German trade union movement. The revival of revolutionary Syndicalism in France had a strong influence on this movement, and this was notably strengthened when the former Social Democrat and later Anarchist, Dr. R. Friedberg came out for the general strike. In 1908 the F.V.D.G. broke completely with Social Democracy and openly professed Syndicalism. After the war this movement took a sharp upswing and in a short time counted 120,000 members. At its congress in Berlin in 1919 the declaration of principles worked out by R. Rocker was adopted; this was in essential agreement with the objectives of the Spanish C.N.T. At the congress in Düsseldorf (1920), the organisation changed its name to *Freie Arbeiter-Union Deutschlands*. The movement carried on an unusually active propaganda and took an especially energetic part in the great actions by organised labour in the Rhenish industrial field. The F.A.U.D. rendered a great service through the tireless labours of its active publishing house, which, in addition to a volumous pamphlet literature, brought out a large number of longer works by Kropotkin, Bakunin, Nettlau, Rocker and others, and by this activity spread the libertarian ideas of these men to wider circles. The movement, in addition to its weekly organ, *Der Syndikalist*, and the theoretical monthly, *Die Internationale*, had at its command a number of local sheets, among them the daily paper, *Die Schöpfung*, in Dusseldorf. After Hitler's accession to power the movement of the German Anarcho-Syndicalists vanished from the scene. A great many of its supporters languished in concentration camps or had to take refuge abroad. In spite of this the organisation still exists in secret, and under most difficult conditions carries on its underground propaganda.

In Sweden there has existed for a long time a very active Syndicalist movement, the *Sveriges Arbetares Centralorganization*, which is also affiliated with the I.W.M.A. This organisation numbers over 40,000 members, which constitutes a very high percentage of the Swedish labour movement.

The internal organisation of the Swedish workers' movement is in very excellent condition. The movement has two daily papers one of them, *Arbetaren*, managed by Albert Jensen in Stockholm. It has its disposal a large number of distinguished propagandists, and has also inaugurated a very active Syndicalist Youth movement. The Swedish Syndicalists take a strong interest in all the workers' struggles in the country. When, on the occasion of the great strike of Adalen, the Swedish government for the first time sent militia against the workers, five men being shot down in the affray, and the Swedish workers replied with a general strike, the Syndicalists played a prominent part, and the government was at last compelled to make concessions to the protest movement of the workers.

In Holland as Syndicalist movement there was the *Nationale Arbeeter-Sekretariat* (N.A.S.), which counted 40,000 members. But when this came more and more under Communist influence, the *Nederlandisch Syndikalistisch Vakverbond* split off from it and announced its affiliation with the I.W.M.A. The most important unit in this new organisation is the metal workers' union under the leadership of A. Rousseau. The movement has carried on, especially in recent years, a very active propaganda, and possesses in *Die Syndikalist*, edited by Albert De Jong, an excellent organ. And the monthly *Grond-Slagen*, which appeared for a few years under the editorship of A. Müller-Lehning, deserves also to be mentioned here. Holland has been from old the classic land of anti-militarism. Domela Neiuwenhuis, former priest and later Anarchist, highly respected by everyone for his pure idealism, in 1904 founded the *Anti-Militarist International*, which, however, had influence worth mentioning only in Holland and France. At the third anti-militarist congress at The Hague (1921) the International *Anti-Militarist Bureau against War and Reaction* was founded, which for the past sixteen years has carried on an extremely active international propaganda group, and has found able and unselfish representatives in men like B de Ligt and Albert de Jong. The bureau was represented at a number of international peace congresses and put out a special press-service in several languages. In 1925 it allied itself with the I.W.M.A. through the *International Anti-military Committee*, and in association with that organisation carries on a tireless struggle against reaction and the peril of new wars.

In addition to these there exist Anarcho-Syndicalist propaganda groups in Norway, Poland and Bulgaria, which are affiliated with the I.W.M.A. Likewise the Japanese *Jiyu Rengo Dantai Zenkoku Kaigi* had entered into formal alliance with the I.W.M.A.

In South America, especially in Argentina, the most advanced country on the southern continent, the young labour movement was from the very beginning strongly influenced by the libertarian ideas of Spanish Anarchism. In 1890 to Buenos Aires from Barcelona came Pellice Parairo, who had lived through the time of the First International and was one of the champions of libertarian Socialism in Spain. Under his influence a congress of trade unions convened in Buenos Aires in 1891, from which arose the *Federación Obrera Argentina*, which at its' fourth congress changed its name to *Federación Obrera Segional Argentina*. The F.O.R.A. has carried on since then without interruption, even though its efficiency was often, as it is again today, disturbed by periods of reaction, and it was driven to underground activity. It is an Anarchist trade union organisation, and it was the soul of all the great labour struggles which have so often shaken that country. The F.O.R.A. began its activity with 40,000 members, which number has grown since the World War to 300,000. Its history, which D. A. de Santiallan has sketched in his work "F.O.R.A.," is one of the most battle-filled chapters in the annals of the international labour movement. For over twenty-five years the movement had a daily paper, *La Protesta*, which under the editorship of Santiallan and Arango, for years published a weekly supplement to which the best minds of international libertarian Socialism contributed. The paper was suppressed after the *coup d'etat* of General Uribura, but it continues to appear in an underground edition oven today, even if not quite daily. Moreover, almost every considerable trade union had its own organ. The F.O.R.A. early joined the I.W.M.A., having been represented at its founding congress by two delegates.

In May, 1929, the F.O.R.A. summoned a congress of all the South American countries, to meet in Buenos Aires. To it the I.W.M.A. sent from Berlin its Corresponding Secretary, A. Souchy. At this congress, besides the F.O.R.A of Argentina, there were represented: Paraguay by the *Centro Obraro del Paraguay*; Bolivia by the *Federacion Local de la Paz, La Antorcha*, and *Luz y Libertad*; Mexico by the *Confederación General de Trabajadores*; Guatemala by the *Comité pro Acción Sindical*; Uruguay by the *Federación Regional Uruguaya*; From Brazil trade unions from seven of the ten constituent states were represented, Costa Rica was represented by the organisation, *Hacia la Libertad*. Even the Chilean I.W.W. sent representatives, although since the dictatorship of Ibanez it had been able to carry on only underground activities. At this congress the *Continental American Workingmen's Association* was brought into existence, constituting the American division of the I.W.M.A. The seat of this organisation was at first in Buenos Aires, but later, because of the dictatorship, it had to be transferred to Uruguay.

These are the forces which Anarcho-Syndicalism at present has at its disposal in the several countries. Everywhere it has to carry on a difficult struggle against reaction as well as against the conservative elements in the present labour movement. Through the heroic battle of the Spanish workers the attention of the world is today directed to this movement, and its adherents are firmly convinced that a great and successful future lies before them.

The Anarchist Library
Anti-Copyright

Rudolf Rocker
Anarcho-syndicalism: Theory and Practice
An Introduction to a Subject Which the Spanish War Has Brought into Overwhelming
Prominence
1938

Retrieved on April 26, 2009 from www.spunk.org
Originally published in 1938 by Martin Secker and Warburg Ltd

theanarchistlibrary.org

Lightning Source UK Ltd.
Milton Keynes UK
UKHW021940090223
416794UK00012B/145